KITCHEN SCIENCE
Lab for Kids

EDIBLE EDITION

52 MOUTH-WATERING RECIPES, AND THE EVERYDAY SCIENCE THAT MAKES THEM TASTE AMAZING

Liz Lee Heinecke

author of
Kitchen Science Lab for Kids

QUARRY

Brimming with creative inspiration, how-to projects, and useful information to enrich your everyday life, Quarto Knows is a favorite destination for those pursuing their interests and passions. Visit our site and dig deeper with our books into your area of interest: Quarto Creates, Quarto Cooks, Quarto Homes, Quarto Lives, Quarto Drives, Quarto Explores, Quarto Gifts, or Quarto Kids.

First published in 2019 by Quarry Books, an imprint of The Quarto Group,
100 Cummings Center, Suite 265-D, Beverly, MA 01915-6101, USA.
T (978) 282-9590 F (978) 283-2742 QuartoKnows.com

Quarry Books titles are also available at discount for retail, wholesale, promotional, and bulk purchase. For details, contact the Special Sales Manager by email at specialsales@quarto.com or by mail at The Quarto Group, Attn: Special Sales Manager, 100 Cummings Center, Suite 265-D, Beverly, MA 01915, USA.

10 9 8 7 6 5 4 3

ISBN: 978-1-63159-741-1

Digital edition published in 2019
eISBN: 978-1-63159-742-8

Library of Congress Cataloging-in-Publication Data

Names: Heinecke, Liz Lee, author.
Title: Kitchen science lab for kids : 52 mouth-watering recipes and the
   everyday science that makes them taste amazing / Liz Heinecke.
Description: Edible edition. | Beverly, MA, USA : Quarry Books, 2019. |
   Includes index. | Audience: Age 8-12.
Identifiers: LCCN 2018053794 | ISBN 9781631597411
Subjects: LCSH: Quick and easy cooking. | Children--Nutrition. | LCGFT:
   Cookbooks.
Classification: LCC TX361.C5 .H45 2019 | DDC 641.5/12--dc23
LC record available at https://lccn.loc.gov/2018053794

Design: Leigh Ring
Photography: Amber Procaccini

Printed in China

ACKNOWLEDGMENTS

Jean Lee, the Julia Child of Manhattan, Kansas, who is a kitchen genius, entrepreneur, teacher, gardener, dietitian, food-safety expert, and my mom.

My dad and physics advisor, Ron Lee.

Ken (my favorite dinner date), our junior chefs, May and Sarah, and Charlie, who considers pizza the most perfect food.

My mother-in-law, Jan Heinecke, Baker of Bars and Queen of Frosting, who has shared many secret family recipes with me.

Photographer Amber Procaccini, who captured the kitchen fun and chaos so beautifully, and the smart, funny, beautiful kids whose smiles light up the pages of this book.

My editors, Jonathan Simcosky and Mary Ann Hall, Nyle Vialet, David Martinell, and the fantastic design team at Quarry Books.

My agents, Peter Knapp and Blair Wilson.

Jennifer, Kari, and Kristine, whose kitchens we invaded for the sake of food science, Susan Nackers, and all of the parents who helped by driving kids and washing dishes during photo shoots.

Zoë François, Michelle Gayer, Molly Herrmann, Tim McKee, and Andrew Zimmern, who wrote words of wisdom about food, science, and creativity for this book.

Cookbooks, columns, and chefs whose recipes I've used and adapted through the years: Alice Waters, *Barefoot Contessa at Home* by Ina Garten, *Better Homes and Gardens New Cookbook* (1976 edition), *Cook's Illustrated*, *How to Cook Everything* by Mark Bittman, Donna Nordin, *Jerusalem: A Cookbook* by Yotam Ottolenghi and Sami Tamimi, Julia Child, Marcella Hazan, the *New York Times* Food section, *Recipes from the Cook's Workshop* (unpublished recipe collection) by Jean Lee, and the *Sunset Pasta Cook Book*.

The food-science books that I referred to extensively while writing this: *Foods: A Scientific Approach* by Helen Charley and Connie Weaver and *The Kitchen as Laboratory* edited by Cesar Vega, Job Ubbink, and Erik Van der Linden.

DEDICATION

To my mom, Jean Hanson Lee, who taught me the joy of cooking and eating good food with friends and family.

CONTENTS

COURSE 06

SASSY SIDES — 80

COURSE 07

BOSSY CAKES, PERFECT PASTRIES, AND FABULOUS FROSTINGS AND FILLINGS — 90

COURSE 08

DARING DECORATIONS AND DELECTABLE DESSERTS — 126

INTRODUCTION

EVERY TIME YOU STEP INTO YOUR KITCHEN TO COOK OR BAKE, YOU PUT SCIENCE TO WORK

In fact, physics and chemistry come into play whenever you simmer, steam, bake, freeze, boil, purée, or ferment food. Knowing the basics of food science will give you the tools to be the boss of your kitchen, and whether you're baking for friends or auditioning for a cooking show, you'll be ready to take on any challenge with confidence.

Edible Kitchen Science Lab lays out fifty-two delicious ideas for exploring food science in your own kitchen by making everything from healthy homemade snacks to marvelous main dishes and mind-boggling desserts. The recipes are designed to mix and match so that you can pair pasta with your favorite sauce or whip up the perfect frosting for any cake. There are plenty of fun, edible decorations included to make every recipe photo-worthy. Whether you gravitate towards trendy or classic, you'll find something to appeal to both your taste buds and your eyes.

Although most of the recipes in this book are based on food I'm familiar with, it's fun to find ways to incorporate your own tastes and traditions into everything you create. Green sauces like pesto can be turned into chimichurri by substituting different herbs, while homemade panir can be substituded for ricotta, sashaying from curry to lasagna with ease. Design your dream dessert by choosing your favorite frosting, fillings, and decorations to create something as beautiful as it is delicious. Ask your friends and family for their favorite versions of a recipe, and use your knowledge of food science to combine them into a dish that suits your taste and cooking style.

The Science Behind the Food section included with each recipe will help you understand the science concepts and nutrition behind the dishes. You'll learn how acids like vinegar and lemon juice enhance flavors, how flour and eggs trap steam to make popovers pop and how crystals form in ice cream. Before long, you'll have the confidence to throw together a feast, bake and decorate show-worthy cakes, or use what you've learned to create your own recipes.

Let's get cooking!

OVERVIEW

THE FIFTY-TWO LABS IN THIS BOOK WILL HAVE YOU EXPERIMENTING WITH FOOD, IN NO TIME WITH DELICIOUS RESULTS.

Each lab contains instructions along with an easy-to-understand explanation of the science behind the food that introduces vocabulary and ideas you can apply to other recipes. The labs are set up to make exploring food science as simple as following a recipe, with the following sections:

→ **INGREDIENTS:** lists all the ingredients you'll need

→ **CHALLENGE LEVEL:** labs with one chef's hat don't require much time or concentration; labs with more hats will challenge your culinary skills

→ **ALLERGEN ALERTS:** all of the recipes in this book are nut free, but this section will indicate if a recipe contains dairy, eggs, or wheat

→ **EQUIPMENT:** lists all equipment that will help you create each dish (you can improvise as needed—for example, a food processor is similar to a blender)

→ **SAFETY TIPS AND HINTS:** provides common-sense safety guidelines and hints for making things go smoothly

→ **RECIPE:** takes you step by step through making the dish

→ **CREATE AND COMBINE:** gives you food pairings, variations, or ideas for taking the recipe a step or two further to inspire your creativity and sense of culinary adventure

→ **THE SCIENCE BEHIND THE FOOD:** offers simple explanations about different ingredients and how they interact, and information on related topics. Keep in mind that failure and troubleshooting are as important as results when you're tackling a new recipe and will ultimately make you a better cook. Dive in. Measuring, scooping, stirring, and making mistakes are part of every chef's experience. Once you've got a recipe mastered, see what else you can do with it. Use what you've learned to create something entirely new or to improve a dish you've always wanted to tweak.

Here's a list of some basic equipment that's good to have on hand as you cook your way through this book:

→ Medium-sized saucepan with heavy bottom

→ Sauté pan (skillet) with gently sloped sides

→ Sharp knives

→ Rolling pin

→ Cutting boards

→ Blender

→ Baking sheets

→ Digital thermometer

→ Large Pot

→ Microplane grater

→ Measuring cups and spoons or a kitchen scale

→ Sieve

→ Cheesecloth

→ Parchment paper

→ Foil

→ Plastic wrap

→ Dish towels

→ Sifter

RULES OF KITCHEN AND FOOD SAFETY

(HOW NOT TO SPOIL YOUR FOOD OR YOUR FUN)

HERE ARE SOME RULES TO KEEP YOU AND YOUR FOOD SAFE IN THE KITCHEN.

→ **A. ADULTS** are awesome. Never, ever cook without an adult in the house. *You should double-check with an adult before tackling a recipe and let them know which steps you will need help with (noted in each recipe). Adults must supervise all uses of heat (such as the oven, stove, and microwave) and sharp objects (such as knives) as well as food safety, including clean-up and proper refrigeration.*

→ **B. BEWARE** hot liquids—always use adult supervision. *Heated sugar syrup and other boiling liquids can cause dangerous and painful burns. Adults should remove hot liquids from the stove or microwave and pour them. Kids should keep their distance until liquids have cooled. Use a candy thermometer rather than a finger to check the temperature of any hot liquid.*

→ **C. COVER** bare feet and pull back long hair. *Not only is dangling hair a fire hazard, it's disgusting to find hair in your food. Feet should be covered to avoid burns caused by splashing hot liquids and injuries from dropped kitchen equipment.*

→ **D. DILIGENCE** prevents fires. *Never turn your back*

on the stove or leave a hot oven unattended. Keep hot pads, oven mitts, and potholders away from open flames and burners.

→ **E. ELECTRICAL SAFETY MEASURES** should always be observed. *Keep all cords away from water and electrical appliances away from the sink. Always keep wet hands away from electrical outlets.*

→ **F. FIRE EXTINGUISHERS** are a cook's best friend,

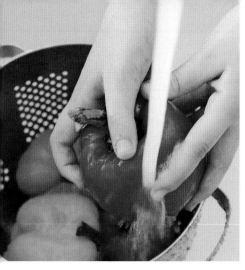

and you should always have one handy in the kitchen. **Remember: an adult should be nearby any time you cook or bake to put out any fire that might occur.** *Never throw water or flour on a grease (fat, butter, or oil) fire. If hot oil catches fire, have an adult cover it with a lid. Salt and baking soda can also be used to put out grease fires.*

→ **G. GERMS** are not your friends. *Although some microbes keep you healthy, many can make you sick, so be mindful of microbes.*

- Hands should be washed with soap before preparing food and re-washed after handling raw meat or eggs. Say the ABCs while washing to ensure 30 seconds of scrubbing.

- Wash raw fruits and vegetables well.

- Don't lick your fingers while preparing food. If you sneeze, turn away from the food and cover your sneeze with your arm.

- Keep perishable foods like meat and dairy in the refrigerator and refrigerate prepared foods, once they've cooled to room temperature.

→ **H. HANDLES IN.** Pot and pan handles should be turned toward the back of the stove when you're not using them, to prevent accidents.

→ **I. INSPECT** the kitchen when you're finished cooking. *Double-check that ovens and burners are turned off and that counters have been wiped down with a soapy rag.*

→ **J. JUST ASK.** If you're not sure something is safe to do on your own, or how to do it, ask an adult for help.

→ **K. KNIVES** are essential to cooking, but even the most experienced chef knows that you must use them correctly and carefully. *All cutting and chopping should be done under adult supervision.*

→ **L. LEARN** from your mistakes. *If a recipe doesn't turn out or you have a kitchen disaster, figure out what went wrong and try it again, or try it a different way. Cooking is science, and many great scientific discoveries and ideas come from experiments that have taken an unexpected turn.*

COURSE
01

DAZZLING DRINKS

Whether entertaining friends or snacking after school, it's fun to sip on a sweet beverage, and you can use science to help you create the perfect thirst-quencher.

BY ADDING LOTS OF SUGAR TO WATER AND HEATING THE MIXTURE, YOU CAN CREATE A SIMPLE SYRUP, WHICH SCIENTIST CALL A "SUPERSATURATED SOLUTION". THESE TASTY SYRUPS CAN BE USED TO SWEETEN AND FLAVOR EVERYTHING FROM TAPIOCA TO CARBONATED WATER.

If you prefer to carbonate your own soda, a microorganism called yeast can help you out. Yeast produce carbon dioxide when they eat sugar, so by mixing water, sugar, yeast and flavoring, you can bottle your own bubbles.

Other tasty beverages in this course include bubble tea, made by rehydrating tapioca pearls, and colorful lemonade density gradients.

"Too often we take beverages for granted . . . it's a shame not to put the same amount of thought and effort into making them as delicious as we do into the food we chew."

Mark Bittman, *How to Cook Everything*

SWEET SODA SYRUPS

INGREDIENTS

→ 3 cups (375 g) fresh or frozen fruit, such as berries, cherries, or mixed fruit

→ 1 tablespoon (15 ml) lemon juice

→ 1 cup sugar (200 g)

→ 1 cup (235 ml) water

EQUIPMENT

→ Large bowl

→ Medium or large saucepan with a heavy bottom

→ Strainer or colander

→ Spoon

→ Stove

SAFETY TIPS AND HINTS

Parental supervision required. To make syrup, you have to get the fruit/sugar mixture very hot, and it can cause burns.

CHALLENGE LEVEL	TIME Around 30 minutes	YIELD 2–3 cups (644–966 g) syrup, depending on fruit

Fig. 6: Sip your homemade soda.

COOK UP FLAVORFUL FRUIT SYRUPS THAT TRANSFORM CARBONATED WATER INTO HOMEMADE SODA POP. IT'S FUN TO EXPERIMENT WITH DIFFERENT COLORS AND FLAVORS.

RECIPE

1. Add the fruit, water, and sugar to the saucepan. **(Fig. 1, 2)**

2. Bring the mixture to a boil over medium-high heat.

3. Stir and boil for about 15–20 minutes, until the fruit is soft enough to crush with a spoon as you cook it. Some kinds of fruit will take longer than others. **(Fig. 3)**

4. Let the mixture cool.

5. Place a colander or strainer over a bowl large enough to hold the contents of the pan. Use a spoon to push the liquid through, collecting it in the bowl underneath. **(Fig. 4)**

6. Add a few tablespoons of the syrup to a glass of carbonated water and stir to make fruit soda. **(Fig. 5)**

7. Sip your homemade soda. **(Fig. 6)**

CREATE AND COMBINE

What flavors can you mix? Which ones have the most color? Use Sweet Soda Syrups to make Sunset Lemonade (Lab 4) or to use in place of the Brown Sugar Simple Syrup to sweeten Boba for your Bodacious Bubble Tea (Lab 3).

Fig. 1: Measure the berries and add them to the saucepan.

Fig. 2: Pour in the water and sugar.

Fig. 3: Cook until the fruit is soft.

Fig. 4: Strain out berries.

Fig. 5: Stir the syrup into carbonated water.

THE SCIENCE BEHIND THE FOOD:

Simple syrups are sweet liquids holding more sugar than water would normally hold at room temperature. Scientists call solutions like these supersaturated.

The heat your stovetop adds to the water makes it possible to dissolve extra sugar molecules, creating a sweet, delicious liquid that can be used to sweeten everything from pancakes to drinks.

RAZZLE-DAZZLE ROOT BEER

INGREDIENTS

→ 1 cup (235 ml) warm (not hot) water

→ 2 cups (400 g) sugar

→ 1 tablespoon (15 ml) root beer or soda pop extract (base)

→ ⅛ heaping teaspoon yeast (champagne, wine, or beer yeast works best, but fresh baker's yeast may be used)

EQUIPMENT

→ 1-gallon (4.5 L) mixing container or large pot

→ Clean, empty plastic soda bottles with caps

→ Labels and pen

→ Large stirring spoon

→ Small bowl

→ Funnel (optional)

CHALLENGE LEVEL	TIME	YIELD
♟♟	30 minutes hands-on, plus 7-10 days to carbonate	1 gallon

Fig. 5: When the bottles feel firm, chill them to enjoy the root beer with friends.

THERE'S NOTHING BETTER THAN AN ICE-COLD MUG OF ROOT BEER, AND IT'S FUN TO BREW YOUR OWN FLAVORFUL BLEND USING YEAST, SUGAR, WATER, AND A SODA BASE. ONCE YOU MASTER ROOT BEER, YOU'LL BE READY TO TACKLE ANY SODA FLAVOR.

SAFETY TIPS AND HINTS

Fermenting root beer bottles can explode if you forget about them and leave them in a warm spot for too long. If the plastic bottle is bulging, or doesn't give at all when you squeeze it, you should throw it away rather than trying to open it.

Follow the instructions in the recipe, continuing to check the bottles periodically once you've moved them to a cooler spot and chilling them in the refrigerator before you open them.

There may be some yeast residue at the bottom of the bottles. It's safe to drink, but pouring carefully will keep it from clouding up your beverage.

RECIPE

1. In a small bowl, completely dissolve ⅛ heaping teaspoon yeast in 1 cup (235 ml) warm water. **(Fig. 1)**

2. Pour 2 cups sugar into a one gallon (4.5 L) container and add enough water to bring the volume to 8 cups. **(Fig. 2)**

3. Shake up the root beer extract and add 1 tablespoon to the sugar/water mix. Stir well.

4. Add 7 cups of water and the yeast mixture from Step 1 to the sugar-water mixture to bring the volume to 1 gallon. Mix well.

5. Fill clean, plastic bottles with the root beer mixture to within 1–2 inches (2.5–5 cm) of the top and screw the caps on tightly. **(Fig. 3)**

6. Add dates and labels to the bottles. **(Fig. 4)**

7. Squeeze the bottles to check how firm they are before fermentation begins.

8. Let the root beer sit at room temperature for 3–5 days, feeling the bottles occasionally to see whether they've become firmer from carbon dioxide gas pressure.

9. When the bottles feel firm, lay them on their side on a baking sheet and store them in a cool, dark place for 1–2 weeks. Then, put them in the refrigerator upright for 1–2 days before opening.

10. Taste your homemade root beer and share it with friends. **(Fig. 5)**

CREATE AND COMBINE
Make some homemade ice cream (Lab 50) and use it to make root beer floats!

Fig. 1: Add yeast to warm water.

Fig. 2: Add sugar and soda extract.

Fig. 3: Fill bottles with mixture..

Fig. 4: Add labels and dates.

THE SCIENCE
BEHIND THE FOOD:

Baker's yeast and brewer's yeast are living organisms called fungi (fun-guy) that are related to mushrooms. Adding water and sugar to dried yeast makes them grow. As they eat sugar, yeast produce carbon dioxide gas in a process called fermentation.

When yeast are warm and growing fast, they produce enough carbon dioxide gas to make bubbles (carbonation) in root beer. The more sugar they eat, the more carbon dioxide they make, and gas pressure builds. That's why you only let the bottles sit at room temperature for a few days before moving them to a cooler spot where the yeast won't grow as fast.

BODACIOUS BUBBLE TEA

INGREDIENTS

BOBA

→ 2 cups (475 ml) water

→ ¼ cup (56 g) boba tapioca pearls

SIMPLE SYRUP

→ 2 cups (300 g) brown sugar

→ 1 cup (235 ml) water

FRUIT SMOOTHIE BUBBLE TEA

→ 1 cup (255 g) frozen fruit

→ 1 cup (235 ml) milk

→ 2 tablespoons sugar (26 g) or honey (40 g)

MATCHA BUBBLE TEA

→ 1 teaspoon matcha powder

→ 1 cup (235 ml) milk

→ 1 cup (140 g) ice

→ 2 tablespoons sugar (26 g) or honey (40 g)

EQUIPMENT

→ 2 medium saucepans

→ Blender

→ Mixing spoon

→ Stove

CHALLENGE LEVEL	ALLERGEN ALERTS Dairy	TIME 30 minutes	YIELD Around 2 cups (475 ml) smoothie or matcha tea

BUBBLE TEA IS A WELL-KNOWN DRINK THAT HAS BEEN POPULAR FOR YEARS. MAKE YOUR OWN VERSION OF THIS DELICIOUS DRINK BY COOKING UP SOME BOBA TO ADD TO YOUR FAVORITE TEA OR SMOOTHIE.

Fig. 5: Make plenty for everyone!

Fig. 1: Cook the boba in water, then rinse and drain.

Fig. 2: Add syrup to sweeten and store boba.

Fig. 3: Blend up a smoothie or some icy matcha tea.

Fig. 4: Add boba to a glass and pour smoothie or tea over boba.

THE SCIENCE
BEHIND THE FOOD:

Tapioca is made from the starchy root of the plant *Manihot esculenta*, commonly called manioc or cassava. The root is peeled, ground, soaked, and roasted to remove poisonous compounds, and gelatinous tapioca is collected during the process. The tapioca is processed to create uniform pearls and then dried.

To make the tapioca the right consistency for bubble tea, it must be rehydrated using water. Boiling allows water to enter the carbohydrate matrix to form the chewy boba jellies that everyone loves.

SAFETY TIPS AND HINTS

Tapioca pearls are a choking hazard for kids under the age of 5.

Adult supervision required for cooking sugar syrups.

Use metal or paper bubble tea straws, if you can find them, since they're better for the environment.

RECIPE

1. Begin by cooking the boba pearls. Boil 2 cups (475 ml) water in a medium saucepan.

2. Add the boba pearls and stir until the tapioca begins to float to the top.

3. Cook the boba over medium heat for 15 minutes, then turn heat off and let them sit for another 15 minutes to keep absorbing water. While the boba sit, make simple syrup (below).

4. Make a simple syrup to sweeten the boba pearls. Add 2 cups (300 g) brown sugar to 1 cup (235 ml) water in a medium saucepan.

5. Boil the mixture until the sugar dissolves. Remove from heat.

6. Rinse and drain the cooked boba. **(Fig. 1)**

7. Add the boba to the simple syrup. They will keep in the refrigerator for at least a week. **(Fig. 2)**

8. Blend together the ingredients for either the Fruit Smoothie Bubble Tea or the Matcha Bubble Tea in the ingredients list. **(Fig. 3)**

9. Add some boba to the bottom of a clear glass and pour the bubble tea mixture over them. Taste the bubble tea. If it needs more sweetness, stir in a little bit of the simple syrup. **(Fig. 4, Fig. 5)**

CREATE AND COMBINE
Could you flavor the boba using Sweet Soda Syrups (Lab 1)? What other smoothie or tea flavors could you combine?

SUNSET LEMONADE

INGREDIENTS

→ Simple syrup, such as Italian soda beverage syrup, or the syrup from Lab 1, or fruit-flavored pancake syrup

→ Lemonade

→ Carbonated water

→ Raspberries (optional)

EQUIPMENT

→ Clear drinking glass

→ Spoon or straw

SAFETY TIPS AND HINTS

Results may vary, depending on how much sugar is in the syrup you use. Try layering different syrups, fruit juices and sodas. You can add sugar to most beverages to make them denser, so they will sink to the bottom of a glass.

CHALLENGE LEVEL	TIME	YIELD
	15 minutes	Depends on the size of the glass you use

Fig. 5: Taste it!

LOADED WITH SUGAR MOLECULES, SIMPLE SYRUPS CREATE A DRINKABLE DENSITY GRADIENT, SITTING AT THE BOTTOM OF THE GLASS UNTIL YOU MIX THEM IN.

RECIPE

1. Pour some fruit syrup into the bottom of a glass. **(Fig. 1)**

2. Use a spoon or a straw to slowly and carefully layer lemonade on top of the syrup. It works best it you let the liquid run down the side of the glass. **(Fig. 2)**

3. Add just enough fruit syrup (a different color, if you have it) to some carbonated water to tint it a light color. Layer it on top of the lemonade. **(Fig. 3)**

4. Float a piece of fruit on top, if you have it. **(Fig. 4)**

5. Taste your creation. **(Fig. 5)**

6. What other fruit juices, syrups, and sodas could you try? **(Fig. 6)**

CREATE AND COMBINE
Make your own simple syrups (Lab 1) to use in your lemonade.

Fig. 1: Pour fruit syrup into the bottom of a glass.

Fig. 2: Use a spoon to layer lemonade on top of the syrup.

Fig. 3: Add some syrup to carbonated water and layer it on the lemonade.

Fig. 4: Float a piece of fruit on top.

THE SCIENCE BEHIND THE FOOD:

Atoms are the building blocks of matter. Sugar molecules are made up of lots of carbon, oxygen, and hydrogen atoms stuck together.

The number of atoms in a certain volume of a liquid determines the liquid's density. The more atoms per liter a liquid has, the more dense it is. Less-dense liquids float on top of denser ones.

That's why you can float carbonated water with just a tiny bit of sugar on top of more heavily sweetened lemonade that's sitting on a bed of sugar-dense syrup.

Fig. 6: What other syrups, juices, and sodas can you layer?

SCRUMPTIOUS SNACKS

You can use science to make phenomenal snacks.

PLAY WITH VAPOR PRESSURE BY POPPING CORN IN A MICROWAVE OVEN, DEHYDRATE DELICIOUS FRUIT LEATHER, PICKLE SOME MOUTH-PUCKERING CUCUMBERS IN ACETIC ACID, OR WHIP UP SOFT PRETZELS BY BATHING THEM IN BAKING SODA.

A good story makes food more fun. So tell your friends that German soft pretzels were invented when a baker accidentally brushed bread sticks with laundry detergent made of lye. Luckily, a baking soda pretzel bath is safer than lye and initiates the same chemical reaction, giving pretzels a gorgeous brown crust that will have everyone reaching for more.

"Knowing how ingredients play with each other as they are mixed together, or once they go into the oven, is the key to having fun with baking. It allows you to be more creative and experiment with flavors and textures in cookies, cakes, pies and breads."

Zoë François, author of *The New Artisan Bread in Five Minutes a Day* series and chief pastry creator on *zoebakes.com*

LAB 05

PAPER-BAG POPCORN EXPLOSION

INGREDIENTS

→ ⅓ cup (85 g) popcorn kernels (unpopped)

→ 1 teaspoon (5 ml) canola or other vegetable oil

→ Salt

EQUIPMENT

→ 2 paper bags

→ Microwave oven

→ Small bowl (optional)

SAFETY TIPS AND HINTS

Steam and hot oil can cause burns. Use caution when opening the bag.

Popping time will depend on the microwave you are using.

CHALLENGE LEVEL	TIME	YIELD
	5 minutes	8 cups

Fig. 4: Microwave until popping stops. Open the bag carefully.

THE HOT CRUNCH OF POPCORN IS A DELICIOUS WAY TO SATISFY A SALT CRAVING OR MAKE WATCHING A MOVIE AT HOME FEEL MORE SPECIAL. POPPING CORN IN A PAPER BAG IS QUICK AND SIMPLE AND DOESN'T GET ANY DISHES DIRTY, WHICH IS ALWAYS A BONUS.

Fig. 1: Measure the popcorn.

Fig. 2: Add oil and mix.

Fig. 3: Pour the popcorn into a bag and fold the top over.

Fig. 5: Share your snack with a friend.

THE SCIENCE
BEHIND THE FOOD:

Corn is special. Each of its kernels is tightly packed inside a glassy hull that holds up extremely well under pressure. When popcorn is heated to 212°F (100°C), moisture inside the kernels evaporates into water vapor, and gas pressure builds inside.

At around 343°F to 388°F (173°C to 198°C), the hull ruptures and the water vaporizes, inflating the cooked starch as the kernel explodes.

Good popcorn contains just the right amount of moisture and is stored sealed in a moisture-proof container for optimal popping performance.

RECIPE

1. Put one bag inside the other to make a double bag.

2. Pour the popcorn into a small bowl. **(Fig. 1)**

3. Add the oil to the popcorn and mix with a spoon. Alternately, add the popcorn and oil directly to the bag and shake it up. **(Fig. 2)**

4. Pour popcorn and oil into the doubled paper bag and fold the top over. **(Fig. 3)**

5. Microwave on high for 3–4 minutes, until the popping has almost stopped. Open the bag carefully to avoid getting burned by steam. **(Fig. 4)**

6. Share your snack with a friend. **(Fig. 5)**

PRETZEL BREAD STICKS

INGREDIENTS

- → 2 cups (475 ml) warm (not hot) water
- → 1 teaspoon salt
- → ½ cup (75 g) light brown sugar
- → 2 envelopes (14 g) active dry yeast
- → ¼ cup (60 ml) vegetable oil
- → 6 cups (750 g) all-purpose flour
- → Cooking spray or butter
- → ½ cup (110 g) baking soda
- → 1 large egg
- → Kosher salt or flaky salt for topping pretzels

EQUIPMENT

- → 3 or 4 baking sheets
- → Basting brush
- → Knife or kitchen scissors
- → Large, deep skillet
- → Large bowl
- → Oven
- → Paper towels
- → Parchment paper
- → Slotted spoon
- → Small bowl
- → Spoon

CHALLENGE LEVEL	ALLERGEN ALERTS	TIME	YIELD
🐾🐾🐾🐾	Eggs, wheat	2 hours	2-3 dozen pretzel sticks

Fig. 9: Bake the pretzel bread sticks until they're a nutty brown color.

BOILING DOUGH IN BAKING SODA-INFUSED WATER GIVES SOFT PRETZELS THEIR UNIQUE FLAVOR AND COLOR. DEVOUR THESE TREATS WHEN THEY'RE FRESH FROM THE OVEN.

Adapted from *Food & Wine* magazine and a recipe from my mom's cooking school, the Cook's Workshop.

Fig. 1: Add yeast to water and brown sugar.

Fig. 2: Add the dry ingredients.

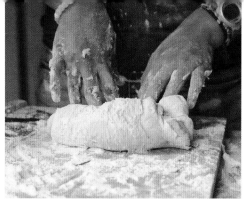
Fig. 3: Knead the dough on a floured board.

SAFETY TIPS AND HINTS

Use caution with boiling water. It's good to have an adult around when you tackle this recipe.

These tasty snacks are easier to handle if you don't make them too big. If your pretzel sticks are falling apart when you boil them, cut them into shorter pieces.

RECIPE

1. Rehydrate the yeast by dissolving ½ cup (75 g) brown sugar in 2 cups (475 ml) warm water and adding the dried yeast. Stir the mixture and let it sit for 5 minutes. **(Fig. 1)**

2. Add ¼ cup vegetable oil to the yeast mixture.

3. Combine ½ teaspoon salt and 3 cups of the flour. Mix well and stir into the yeast and oil mixture. **(Fig. 2)**

4. Use your hands to knead an additional 2 ¾ cups (340 g) of flour into the dough and dump it out onto a flat surface covered with flour.

5. Continue to knead the dough until it is soft and silky, adding the remaining ¼ cup flour if needed so the dough is not too sticky to work with. **(Fig. 3)**

6. Coat a large bowl with vegetable oil. Add the dough and let it rise at room temperature until it has doubled in size (30–45 minutes, depending on the temperature).

7. Preheat your oven to 450°F (230°C).

8. Line baking sheets with parchment paper that has been greased with cooking spray or butter.

9. Punch down the pretzel dough and knead it a few times. Flatten it out and cut it into 24 pieces of similar size. **(Fig. 4, 5)**

10. Roll each piece into sticks around ½ inch thick, then cut each pretzel stick in half. Position them on the parchment on the baking sheets with space for them to double in size. Let them rise for 25 minutes. **(Fig. 6)**

11. While they rise, beat an egg and 1 tablespoon water in a small bowl to create an egg wash for the pretzels.

12. Bring 2 quarts of water and ½ cup baking soda to a simmer in a deep skillet. Reduce the heat to medium. Put some paper towels on a large plate for draining bread sticks.

13. Use slotted spoons to transfer 6 to 8 bread sticks to the simmering water. After about 20 seconds, flip them over and simmer for another 20 seconds. **(Fig. 7)**

PRETZEL BREAD STICKS
(CONTINUED)

Fig. 4: Let the dough rise and then punch it down.

Fig. 5: Flatten the dough and cut it into sections.

Fig. 6: Roll out the pretzels and cut them in half.

Fig. 7: Boil the pretzel dough in baking soda and water.

Fig. 8: Score the pretzels and brush them with egg yolk mixture.

Fig. 10: Share your pretzel bread sticks with a friend.

THE SCIENCE
BEHIND THE FOOD:

A chemical reaction called the Maillard reaction gives food such as cookies, bread crust, seared steak, and soft pretzels their beautiful golden-brown color and rich flavor. Also called the "browning reaction," the Maillard reaction occurs when certain sugars, called reducing sugars, and amino acids (the building blocks for proteins) are heated together.

Increasing the pH value of food—that is, making it less acidic—by adding baking soda speeds up the Maillard reaction. When you make pretzels, boiling the dough in baking soda and water, and brushing it with egg proteins creates perfect conditions for a gorgeous caramel finish.

The first Bavarian pretzels were made by accident in 1939, when a German Baker mistakenly glazed his pretzels with lye (sodium hydroxide) instead of sugar water. The results were delicious.

4. Drain the boiled sticks on the paper towels and return them to the parchment paper on the baking sheets. Continue boiling the remaining pretzel sticks. When you're about halfway through, add a cup of hot water to the cooking liquid to replenish it.

5. Snip or score the tops of the pretzels lightly, brush them with egg wash, and sprinkle them with salt. Bake them at 450˚F (230˚C) for 10 minutes or until they're a rich brown color. **(Fig. 8, 9)**

16. Enjoy the soft pretzels plain or serve them with your favorite dipping sauce. **(Fig. 10)**

CREATE AND COMBINE

Make homemade pesto (Lab 20), aioli (Lab 16), or hummus (Lab 17) to take your pretzel dip to the next level.

LAB 07

FLAVORFUL FRUIT LEATHER

INGREDIENTS

→ 3 cups (435 g) fresh or frozen chopped fruit, such as strawberries, blueberries, raspberries, mango, or peaches

→ 1 tablespoon (15 ml) lemon juice

→ 1–4 tablespoons (20–80 g) honey

→ ¼ cup (60 ml) water (optional, depending on fruit)

EQUIPMENT

→ Baking sheet

→ Fork

→ Kitchen shears or clean scissors (optional)

→ Saucepan

→ Standard or immersion blender (optional)

→ Silicone mat or parchment paper

→ Stove

→ Wooden spoon

→ Plastic bag with end cut off, for piping (optional)

CHALLENGE LEVEL	TIME	YIELD
🔴🔴	30 minutes hands-on, plus 2–3 hours drying time	1–2 dozen pieces of fruit leather, depending on fruit and design

Fig. 5: You've made fruit leather!

YOU WON'T BE ABLE TO STOP EATING THESE NATURALLY SWEET FRUIT SNACKS! WRAP THEM IN PARCHMENT TO MAKE HOMEMADE FRUIT ROLL-UPS OR CUT THEM INTO CREATIVE SHAPES BEFORE YOU GOBBLE THEM UP.

SAFETY TIPS AND HINTS

Hot fruit leather can cause burns. Let it cool before you taste it.

Silicone mats work better than parchment for drying fruit leather, but you can use either.

Frozen mango is our family's favorite fruit for fruit leather.

Make several batches of fruit leather at once to create multiple flavors and colors.

Some fruit combinations dry out more quickly than others. Fruit leather like mango that dries quickly can be removed from the pan while other fruit purée continues to dry in the oven.

RECIPE

1. Preheat the oven to its lowest setting, such as 170°F (77°C).

2. Place the chopped fruit and lemon juice in a saucepan.

3. Add honey to the fruit. Fruit such as blueberries and strawberries tastes better with more honey, while peaches and mango require less. **(Fig. 1)**

4. Cook the fruit over medium heat, stirring occasionally until most of the water evaporates and it is thick like jam. The fruit should be soft enough to crush with a fork. Some fruit that contains less water, such as mango, will require the addition of $\frac{1}{4}$ cup water as you cook it. **(Fig. 2)**

5. Remove the fruit mixture from the heat and allow it to cool.

6. When fruit is at room temperature, transfer it to a mixing bowl and use a fork or a blender to mash it into a smooth paste.

7. Taste the mixture to see whether it needs more honey. It should be tart, but flavorful. Add another tablespoon of honey, if needed.

8. Spread or pipe the fruit mixture onto a silicone baking sheet or parchment that has been placed on a baking sheet. Use a knife or spatula to spread it into a thin layer. **(Fig. 3)**

9. Put the fruit in the oven to dry until it is no longer sticky to the touch. **(Fig. 4)**

10. When it is dry, peel the fruit leather off the silicone sheet or parchment. Roll it up in parchment or cut it into fun shapes. Try to eat it within a week or so of making it. **(Fig. 5)**

CREATE AND COMBINE

Experiment with different types and mixtures of fruit. Do some fruits contain more water than others? Sour fruits naturally contain more acid than fruits with more delicate flavors, so adding them to sweet fruits will create a tasty mixture.

Fig. 1: Add honey to the fruit.

Fig. 2: Cook over medium heat.

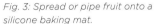

Fig. 3: Spread or pipe fruit onto a silicone baking mat.

Fig. 4: Dry the fruit leather in the oven until it is no longer sticky.

 # THE SCIENCE BEHIND THE FOOD:

Microorganisms, such as bacteria and fungi, need water to grow and multiply. Fresh foods such as fruit, meat, and dairy contain lots of water and allow microbes to grow easily, providing nutrients as well. Although fruit is protected by its skin, most kinds will start to spoil after a few days of sitting at room temperature.

Removing water is an ancient method of food preservation and makes it possible to store everything from fish to figs at room temperature. Dehydrating (drying) fruit removes enough water to prevent microbes from growing. The sugar in fruit and honey also discourages bacteria.

PUCKER-UP PICKLES

INGREDIENTS

→ Small cucumbers

→ Onion or garlic (optional)

→ Large container of white vinegar, cider vinegar, or rice vinegar

→ Salt

→ Sugar

EQUIPMENT

→ Cutting board

→ Mixing spoon

→ Knife

→ Small jars

SAFETY TIPS AND HINTS

Use proper cutting technique, keeping fingers and thumbs tucked away from the knife end of the vegetable you're cutting.

If using cider or rice vinegar, reduce the amount of sugar by half.

CHALLENGE LEVEL	TIME 30 minutes	YIELD This recipe makes 2 cups (475 ml) of pickling vinegar, but you can double, triple, or quadruple it, depending on how many cucumbers you want to pickle

VINEGAR IS DILUTED ACETIC ACID AND IS GOOD AT PRESERVING AND FLAVORING FOOD. TAKE THE EDGE OFF THE ACIDITY WITH SOME SUGAR AND POUR IT OVER SLICED CUCUMBERS TO MAKE QUICK REFRIGERATOR PICKLES THAT LIVEN UP PICNICS AND SUMMERTIME BARBECUES.

Fig. 5: Pair your pickles with a snack.

Fig. 1: Slice cucumbers into spears or coins.

Fig. 2: Pack the cucumbers tightly into jars.

Fig. 3: Pour the vinegar solution over the cucumbers.

Fig. 4: Screw the lids on loosely.

THE SCIENCE
BEHIND THE FOOD:

Acids such as citric acid and vinegar taste sour and are often added to food to balance and brighten flavor. They can also be used to preserve food in a process called pickling.

The scientific name for vinegar is acetic acid, and store-bought vinegar is diluted with enough water to make it safe to consume. Not only does it taste sour and kill microbes, it inactivates chemicals that can interact with oxygen to turn veggies brown, keeping pickled veggies looking pretty.

RECIPE

1. Slice cucumbers into coins or spears. **(Fig. 1)**

2. Pack them tightly into jars. Add onion or garlic, if desired. **(Fig. 2)**

3. Mix 2 cups (475 ml) vinegar, 2 teaspoons salt, and 8 teaspoons (36 g) sugar. Stir until the sugar dissolves.

4. Pour the vinegar mixture over the cucumbers. Make more vinegar solution if you need it, or top jars off with plain vinegar. Screw the jar lids on loosely. **(Fig. 3, 4)**

5. Refrigerate pickles for 1–2 days. Pair them with a snack or pile them on a sandwich. **(Fig. 5)**

CREATE AND COMBINE

Make some pretzels (Lab 6) to go with your pickles.

To make Southern-style pickles, slice cucumbers very thin, sprinkle them with salt and let them sit for half an hour. Dry them with a paper towel, and add them to the vinegar-sugar mixture. Refrigerate and serve them as an appetizer.

Pickle other veggies, such as thinly sliced onions. Experiment with different seasonings.

JUICY FRUIT SPAGHETTI AND POPPING BOBA

INGREDIENTS

→ ¾ cup (175 ml) fruit juice, such as mango/orange juice (no added calcium)

→ ¼ teaspoon sodium alginate

→ 2 teaspoons calcium chloride

→ 4 cups (946 ml) water, plus extra

EQUIPMENT

→ 2 large bowls

→ Blender, hand blender, or wire whisk)

→ Medium bowl

→ Mixing spoon or whisk

→ Slotted spoon

→ Squeeze bottle or medium to large syringe

CHALLENGE LEVEL	TIME	YIELD
🍳🍳🍳	1 hour hands-on, plus 2 hours to overnight refrigeration	¾ cup (175 ml) fruit juice/sodium alginate mixture for making boba or fruit spaghetti

Fig. 5: Garnish and enjoy!

USE TECHNOLOGY ADAPTED FROM SCIENTIFIC RESEARCH LABS TO POLYMERIZE TASTY FRUIT SPAGHETTI AND POPPING BOBA.

SAFETY TIPS AND HINTS

You'll have to order some of the ingredients for this one, and you'll need a squeeze bottle or syringe, but it's so much fun that it's worth it.

Fruit juice containing too much calcium will solidify immediately when you add the sodium alginate, so it's a good idea to have a few different juice options on hand.

RECIPE

1. Pour ¾ cup fruit juice into a medium bowl and refrigerate for 30 minutes. This will help dissolve the alginate in step 2.

2. Blend or whisk the cold juice and sprinkle the sodium alginate into the agitated liquid. Mix well, trying to minimize bubbles. The liquid may thicken slightly. **(Fig. 1)**

3. Put the liquid in the refrigerator and let it sit for 2 hours to overnight, to remove bubbles.

4. When the alginate mixture is ready, fill a large bowl with water.

5. Add the calcium chloride to the water and whisk it in until dissolved, creating a calcium chloride bath. **(Fig. 2)**

6. Fill the syringe or squeeze bottle with the juice/sodium alginate mixture and try to drip the juice into the calcium chloride bath one drop at a time to form popping boba, also called spherified caviar. **(Fig. 3)**

7. Let the boba sit in the bath for 1–3 minutes and remove them using a slotted spoon.

8. Fill a bowl with clean water and use it to rinse the boba.

9. To make fruit spaghetti, squeeze a continuous stream of fruit juice solution into the calcium chloride bath. Let sit until firm and then remove and rinse as before. **(Fig. 4)**

10. Taste your creation. Boba and fruit spaghetti can be stored in fruit juice without sodium alginate. **(Fig. 5)**

CREATE AND COMBINE
Add popping boba to a fruit smoothie or frozen matcha tea (Lab 3).

Experiment with different juices to see which ones work best for making popping boba and fruit spaghetti.

Fig. 1: Blend sodium alginate into juice.

Fig. 2: Add calcium chloride to the water.

Fig. 3: Use a syringe or squeeze bottle to make popping boba.

Fig. 4: Thick juice solution makes great fruit spaghetti.

THE SCIENCE
BEHIND THE FOOD:

Sodium alginate (say it like you say *algae*!) is a substance found in the cell walls of brown algae, including seaweed and kelp. Its rubbery, gel-like consistency may be important for the flexibility of seaweed, which gets tossed around on ocean waves.

Here on dry land, you can use sodium alginate to make balloon-like blobs and spaghetti-like strands from fruit juice. We can thank scientists for this delicious project, since they discovered that a chemical reaction between sodium alginate and calcium causes sodium alginate to polymerize, forming a gel. In this experiment, the gel forms on the outside of a sodium alginate fruit juice blob, where the chemical reaction is taking place. The inside remains liquid!

COURSE
O3

CREAMY CHEESE AND FAB FERMENTS

FERMENTATION IS A CHEMICAL PROCESS INVOLVED IN THE BREAKDOWN OF CERTAIN SUBSTANCES BY MICROORGANISMS, INCLUDING BACTERIA AND YEASTS.

From cheese to pickles, microbes have helped humans craft food for thousands of years, but scientists are just beginning to understand the impact of beneficial bacteria on human health. Eating fermented foods such as yogurt and lacto-fermented vegetables may help keep our guts populated with good bacteria, crowding out microbes that can make us sick.

Tangy yogurt and silky crème fraîche are two tasty fermented dairy products that are easy to make at home. Throw some fermented green beans into the mix, and you've got a fermentation station. Pair pickles with some crackers and homemade cheese to create a nutritious, delicious snack platter.

Unfermented cheese can be made faster than fermented cheese by breaking up milk's delicate suspension of water, fat, and proteins to create curds that can be cut, stretched, or cooked into a curry.

"I teach a lot of cooking classes, and one of the things that interests our guests is the "why" of doing something a certain way in the kitchen. Cooking is not just about passion and creativity, but using the science of ingredients to create."

Molly Herrmann, owner and executive chef of Kitchen in the Market, a shared commercial kitchen and cooking school in Minneapolis, MN.

STRETCHY MOZZARELLA

INGREDIENTS

→ 1¼ cup (300 ml) water

→ ⅛ teaspoon lipase (optional)

→ ¼ teaspoon calcium chloride (optional)

→ ¼ teaspoon (150 g) rennet or ¼ rennet tablet

→ 1½ teaspoons citric acid

→ 1 gallon (4.5 L) milk

→ ½ teaspoon salt

EQUIPMENT

→ Instant-read thermometer

→ Long knife

→ Large pot or pan with lid

→ Microwave-safe container

→ Microwave oven

→ Mixing spoon

→ Slotted spoon

→ Small mixing bowls

→ Stove

CHALLENGE LEVEL 🎩🎩🎩	ALLERGEN ALERTS Dairy	TIME 1 hour or so, start to finish	YIELD Around 1 pound (455 g) mozzarella

THERE'S SOMETHING SATISFYING ABOUT CONJURING CHEESE FROM A CARTON OF MILK. THIS SIMPLE MOZZARELLA IS FUN TO STRETCH, SHAPE, AND SNACK ON.

Adapted from thekitchn.com and advice from Midwest Brewing Supply.

Fig. 5: Stretch and fold the curds.

RECIPE

1. If using calcium chloride and lipase, add both to ½ cup (120 ml) cool water and stir. If not using calcium chloride and lipase, put aside ½ cup (120 ml) water for Step 6.

2. In another small container, add the rennet to ¼ cup (60 ml) water. **(Fig. 1)**

3. In a seperate bowl, add the citric acid to ½ cup (120 ml) water.

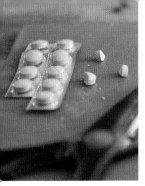
Fig. 1: Add rennet to water.

Fig. 2: Heat the milk to 90°F (32°C).

Fig. 3: After curds form, cut them into a grid.

Fig. 4: Remove the curds from the liquid whey.

Fig. 6: Melt the mozzarella on pizza or add it to a salad.

SAFETY TIPS AND HINTS

Do not use ultra-pasteurized milk to make cheese. Regular pasteurized milk will work fine.

You can purchase cheese-making supplies online or at a bricks-and-mortar brewing supply store.

Rennet, the set of enzymes used to make milk into cheese, is generally not vegetarian, but you can get vegetarian versions that will work to make mozzarella. Read the label to see how much to add per gallon of milk. Cut tablets with kitchen shears, not a knife.

THE SCIENCE BEHIND THE FOOD:

It takes chemistry to transform milk into mozzarella, which is called a pasta filata, or stretched paste, cheese.

Milk contains a unique group of proteins called caseins, and some casein molecules have tails that cling to water, keeping them suspended in milk, along with fat and other milk proteins. Heating milk and adding acid creates the right conditions for rennet, a chemical called an enzyme, to chop the tails off the caseins. Without tails, the caseins lose their love for water and clump together, trapping fat and some water to create curds.

One advantage of using rennet instead of a harsher acid like lemon juice to make cheese is that it creates a more neutral environment. This allows specific microbial cultures to be grown in cheese for extra flavor.

4. Pour the milk into the large pot or pan. Add the citric acid solution from Step 3.

5. Stirring over medium-high heat, bring the milk to 90°F (32°C) and remove from the heat. **(Fig. 2)**

6. Add the calcium chloride/lipase solution or water from Step 1. Add the rennet solution from Step 2 and stir the mixture for 30 seconds.

7. Stop stirring, cover the pot, and let the mixture rest for 5 minutes.

8. With a knife, cut the curds in the pot into a grid and set them back on the stove, heating them to 105°F (41°C), stirring gently so the curds stay together. **(Fig. 3)**

9. Remove the pan from the heat and stir carefully for another 5 minutes.

10. Use the slotted spoon to move the curds out of the pot and into a microwave-safe container. **(Fig. 4)**

11. Microwave the curds on high for 1 minute and pour off any liquid. Use a spoon to fold them over a few times.

12. Microwave the curds for another 30 seconds and repeat until they reach 135°F (57°C).

13. Sprinkle the salt over the curds, and when the cheese is cool enough to touch, fold the curds over, stretch them, and repeat. **(Fig. 5)**

14. As you work the cheese, the texture should change; the cheese will feel harder to stretch and look glossy.

15. When the cheese is ready, mold it into several small balls, or one big one. Store it in the refrigerator until you eat it.

CREATE AND COMBINE
Cut mozzarella up to put on pizza (Lab 25), snack on it with pretzel bread sticks (Lab 6), or serve it with fresh tomatoes and basil, drizzled with olive oil and balsamic vinegar. **(Fig. 6)**

INGREDIENTS

→ 1 gallon (4.5 L) whole milk (not ultra-pasteurized)

→ ¼ cup (60 ml) fresh lemon juice, and more as needed (2-3 lemons)

EQUIPMENT

→ Cheesecloth

→ Colander or sieve

→ Large pot

→ Stirring spoon

SAFETY TIPS AND HINTS

Keep adding lemon juice until you see nice curds forming in the liquid.

CHALLENGE LEVEL	ALLERGEN ALERTS	TIME	YIELD
🍳🍳	Dairy	30 minutes hands-on, plus time to drain overnight	Around 1 pound (455 g) panir

Fig. 6: Pair panir with green sauce, add it to curry, or put it in lasagna.

IT'S SIMPLE TO MAKE CHEESE AT HOME BY HEATING MILK AND ADDING LEMON JUICE. AFTER DRAINING THE CHEESE, ADD IT TO CURRY, DRIZZLE OLIVE OIL OVER IT, OR LAYER IT INTO LASAGNA.

RECIPE

1. Juice 2 or 3 lemons. **(Fig. 1)**

2. Pour the milk into a large pot.

3. Heat the milk, stirring constantly until bubbles start to form around the edge of the pot, just before it boils. **(Fig. 2)**

4. Add ¼ cup (60 ml) of lemon juice, turn the heat down, and stir until curds form, separating from the greenish liquid called whey. If curds don't form, add more lemon juice. **(Fig. 3)**

5. Put a double layer of cheesecloth on the colander. Scoop out the curds and put them on the cheesecloth to drain. Squeeze out the excess whey. **(Fig. 4)**

6. Set the cheese in the cheesecloth back on a colander and position the plate and a weight (preferably a 28 oz can) on top. Cover with plastic and put it in the refrigerator overnight to finish draining.

7. Cut the panir into pieces and taste it. Eat it with fruit or olive oil and salt. You can also add it to a curry, use it to fill pasta shells or make lasagna. **(Fig. 5, 6)**

Fig. 1: Juice the lemons.   Fig. 2: Stir the milk over heat.

Fig. 3: Add lemon juice and stir until curds form.

THE SCIENCE
BEHIND THE FOOD:

Milk is made up mostly of water, but it also contains fat, proteins, carbohydrates, vitamins, and minerals. It's an emulsion (mixture) of fat globules, and proteins called caseins, suspended in liquid milk. Cheese-making is the process of separating the water from the fats and certain proteins to create the gel-like substance we call cheese.

Acidifying milk with lemon juice changes the chemistry, destroying the emulsion, which causes the fats and caseins to clump together in curds. The leftover whey contains some proteins and most of the water.

Fig. 4: Scoop out the curds and drain them on cheesecloth.   Fig. 5: Cut cheese into pieces.

COOL CRÈME FRAÎCHE

INGREDIENTS

→ 1 cup (235 ml) heavy cream

→ 1 tablespoon (15 ml) cultured buttermilk (not ultra-pasteurized)

EQUIPMENT

→ Dish towel or plate

→ Microwave-safe bowl or jar, or small saucepan if not using a microwave

→ Microwave oven or stove

→ Mixing spoon

→ Thermometer

SAFETY TIPS AND HINTS

After adding the buttermilk, cover the dish loosely with a dish towel or plate to keep unwanted microbes from drifting into your crème fraîche.

CHALLENGE LEVEL	ALLERGEN ALERTS	TIME	YIELD
♟	Dairy	5 minutes hands-on, plus sitting overnight	1 cup (224 g) crème fraîche

THIS RICH, SMOOTH CULTURED DAIRY DELIGHT IS PERFECT FOR SWIRLING INTO SOUPS, WHISKING INTO SAUCES, DRIZZLING OVER ROASTED POTATOES, OR ADDING TO DIPS. BECAUSE IT PAIRS WITH BOTH SAVORY AND SWEET, CRÈME FRAÎCHE IS FABULOUS ON FRUIT AS WELL.

Fig. 6: Or use instead of sour cream.

Fig. 1: Measure cream.

THE SCIENCE
BEHIND THE FOOD:

Buttermilk is made by mixing cream with certain bacterial cultures that produce lactic acid when they grow.

As crème fraîche sits at room temperature and buttermilk bacteria multiply, the acidic environment acts on proteins in the cream, thickening the liquid. Lactic acid also gives crème fraîche its tangy flavor, which is enhanced by other flavor- and aroma-enhancing compounds produced by the bacteria.

RECIPE

1. Pour 1 cup (235 ml) heavy cream into a microwave-safe container or saucepan. **(Fig. 1)**

2. Warm the cream to just above room temperature, but not above 85°F (29°C). If heating in the microwave, this should take about 30 seconds; if heating on the stove, use low heat. **(Fig. 2)**

3. Check the temperature of the cream. Let it cool to 85°F (29°C), if necessary. **(Fig. 3)**

4. Add 1 tablespoon buttermilk to the warm cream and stir. **(Fig. 4)**

5. Loosely cover the mixture with the dish towel or plate and let it sit at room temperature for 12–36 hours, until it thickens. When it's ready, store it in a covered container in the refrigerator until you use it.

6. You can mix crème fraîche with pesto or herbs to make a dip. **(Fig. 5)**

7. It's delicious drizzled over roasted vegetables like potatoes. **(Fig. 6)**

CREATE AND COMBINE
Make roasted potatoes (Lab 31) to serve with your crème fraîche.

Whip the crème fraîche with a spoonful of sugar and serve it on fruit pie. (Lab 37).

Fig. 2: Warm the cream.

Fig. 3: Let the cream cool.

Fig. 4: Add the buttermilk to the warm cream and stir.

Fig. 5: You can mix crème fraîche with pesto or herbs to make a dip.

YUMMIEST YOGURT

INGREDIENTS

→ 2 quarts (1.9 L) pasteurized whole or 2% milk (preferably not ultra-pasteurized)

→ ¼ cup (60 ml) heavy whipping cream (optional)

→ 4 tablespoons (60 g) plain yogurt containing live active cultures

EQUIPMENT

→ Cheesecloth and a colander for thickening yogurt (optional)

→ Large saucepan or pot with heavy bottom and lid

→ Medium bowl

→ Oven with an oven light

→ Stove

→ Thermometer, such as an instant-read thermometer

→ Whisk

CHALLENGE LEVEL	ALLERGEN ALERTS	TIME	YIELD
🔲🔲	Dairy	30 minutes hands-on, plus 6-12 hours for incubation	2 quarts yogurt

Adapted from the *New York Times* Food Section

Fig. 4: Mix in some jam to sweeten yogurt.

USE THE WARMTH OF AN OVEN LIGHT TO INCUBATE SMOOTH, TANGY HOMEMADE YOGURT THAT CAN BE EATEN PLAIN OR SWEETENED WITH JAM. YOGURT MAKES A SMOOTH SOUR CREAM SUBSTITUTE AND A CREAMY BASE FOR DIPS.

Yogurt is created when certain safe, edible bacteria grow in warm milk. To make yogurt, you must choose yogurt containing live cultures as a starter. The yogurt label should say "live active yogurt cultures."

Cover the yogurt culture once you've added the starter to keep unwanted bacteria away and refrigerate it following the incubation.

RECIPE

1. Rinse out a pan with cold water to chill the metal.

2. Add milk to the pan. Pour in ¼ cup cream, if desired, and heat the mixture on medium-high.

3. Stir the milk as it warms and check the temperature occasionally until it comes to a simmer. **(Fig. 1)**

4. When the milk reaches 180°F to 200°F (82°C to 93°C), turn off the stove and remove the pot from the heat.

5. Let the milk cool to 110°F (43°C) so it won't kill the bacteria in your starter culture.

6. Add ½ cup (120 ml) of the warm milk to a bowl containing 4 tablespoons of yogurt. Whisk well. **(Fig. 2)**

7. Stir the milk/yogurt mixture into the pot of warm milk and put a lid on the pot.

8. Place the pot in the oven with the oven light on for 6-12 hours. Move it to the refrigerator for at least 4 hours. The longer yogurt sits in the oven, the thicker it will be.

9. Taste the yogurt. If you'd like thicker yogurt, line a colander with cheesecloth, set it over a bowl, and spoon the yogurt onto the cheesecloth. Refrigerate, scraping the cheesecloth with a spoon occasionally, until it reaches the desired thickness. **(Fig. 3)**

10. Enjoy your homemade yogurt! Stir in some jam, eat it plain on a taco, or make a dip by adding cucumber, dill, and lemon juice! **(Fig. 4, 5)**

CREATE AND COMBINE
Season the yogurt with your favorite herb and drizzle it over some roasted carrots (Lab 30).

Add pesto (Lab 20) to your yogurt to create a flavorful dip for fresh veggies.

Fig. 1: Heat the milk and cream.

Fig. 2: Whisk the yogurt into the warm milk.

Fig. 3: You can thicken the yogurt to make Greek-style yogurt..

Fig. 5: Adding cucumbers, fresh dill, and salt makes delicious dip.

THE SCIENCE
BEHIND THE FOOD:

Microbes create the most delicious foods, and scientists have discovered that many of them are good for your gut. Heat-loving bacteria such as Lactobacillus acidophilus are called thermophiles. They eat the sugars in milk and grow quickly at the right temperatures, crowding out unwanted bacteria.

As they break down milk sugar, yogurt bacteria produce lactic acid, which gives yogurt a delicious, tangy flavor. Proteins in the milk unravel and are chopped into smaller pieces during the yogurt-making process, creating a colloid (gel), which is why the yogurt thickens as it sits. Because the milk proteins have been broken down, yogurt can be easier to digest than milk.

TANGY GREEN BEANS AND CARROTS

INGREDIENTS

→ Fresh green beans and/or carrots

→ 8 cups (1.9 L) water (filtered if possible)

→ 4 tablespoons (75 g) non-iodized salt, such as pickling salt or kosher salt

→ Dill (washed well) (optional)

→ Garlic cloves (optional)

EQUIPMENT

→ Clean jars (run through dishwasher on sanitize cycle, if possible) with lids

→ Cutting board

→ Garlic press (optional)

→ Knife

→ Vegetable scrubber (optional)

→ Vegetable peeler (optional)

CHALLENGE LEVEL	TIME	YIELD
	30 minutes hands-on, plus 2 weeks for pickling	8 cups fermenting liquid (salt water)

Fig. 6: Use another jar or drinking glass as a weight.

FERMENTING IS FUN! USE MICROBE POWER TO PICKLE CARROT STICKS AND GREEN BEANS IN SALT WATER.

RECIPE

1. Peel the carrots (if using) and cut them into sticks about ½ inch (1 cm) thick. Snap the ends off green beans.

2. If using garlic, peel several cloves and boil them in water for 30 seconds. You can add them to the jars later for extra flavor.

3. Wash all vegetables well with water.

4. Snap green beans and trim carrots so that they'll fit into the jars on end, leaving about 1¼ inches (3 cm) of head room at the top of the jar. **(Fig. 1)**

5. Pack the carrot sticks and beans into jars as tightly as possible so that they will stay under the brine and not float up. It will help to lay the jars on their sides as you pack them. Squeeze dill and a clove of garlic into each jar, if you have prepared them. **(Fig. 2, 3, 4)**

6. Make a pickling brine by dissolving 4 tablespoons of salt in 8 cups of water. Use filtered water if you have it, but tap water will work too.

7. Pour the brine over the vegetables until they are submerged. Leave around ¾ inch (2 cm) of space at the top of the jar. You can use another jar as a weight to keep the vegetables submerged. **(Fig. 5, 6)**

8. Put lids on the jars loosely and put the jars on a plate or baking sheet.

9. Let the brined vegetables sit at room temperature for 24 hours. Watch for bubbles to form.

10. After 24 hours, remove the lids to "burp" the jars. Replace the lids and let sit another 24 hours.

11. Burp the jars again by opening the lids. Set them on a paper towel on a shelf in the door of your refrigerator and let them sit for another week or two.

12. Taste the pickles. They should be salty and slightly sour. You can chop them up and add them to other food, or eat them plain.

13. Store the tangy pickles in your refrigerator for up to 1 month. If they start to look moldy or smell bad, throw them away.

CREATE AND COMBINE
Pair your pickles with some pretzel bread sticks (Lab 6) for a delicious snack.

SAFETY TIPS AND HINTS

Carrot sticks can be tricky to cut. Younger kids should stick to peeling and let an adult do the cutting.

Hold the iodine. To lactoferment, you'll want to use pickling, kosher, or another non-iodized salt.

Pack the beans and carrots tightly so they stay under the brine as they ferment. This will help prevent mold growth.

THE SCIENCE
BEHIND THE FOOD:

Although we can't see them without a microscope, bacteria cover virtually everything around us. Vegetables are no exception, and we can use some of the bacteria on vegetables to make pickles, via a process called lactofermentation.

Bacteria that turn veggies into pickles can grow in high-salt environments that kill most harmful bacteria. Keeping the vegetables under the brine prevents fungi (mold) from growing and helps certain pickling bacteria thrive. As they grow, the bacteria produce lactic acid, making the pickles taste sour. They also give off carbon dioxide gas, which is why you see bubbles and have to "burp" the jars.

Fig. 1: Prep the veggies.

Fig. 2: Pack vegetables into jars.

Fig. 3: Pack them in tightly.

Fig. 4: Add garlic that has been boiled briefly (blanched) and herbs.

Fig. 5: Cover completely with salt water.

COURSE
04

DIVINE DIPS, DRESSINGS, AND SAVORY SAUCES

THIS COURSE TAKES YOU ON A JOURNEY INTO EMULSIONS AND PURÉES. IT'S MAGICAL TO TRANSFORM OIL, VINEGAR, AND MUSTARD FROM A MESSY, IMMISCIBLE (UNMIXABLE) PUDDLE INTO SWIRLS OF SILKY GOLDEN VINAIGRETTE, OR WHIP UP CHEF JULIA CHILD'S MAYONNAISE.

Sauces bring out the best in food. Light sauces enhance food, while heavier ones partner up with foods in a costarring role. Many sauces are made by creating flavorful suspensions and emulsions, so science comes into play each time you mix them up.

Their viscosity (thickness) determines how well they flow, and the proportions of ingredients work together to create a balanced flavor.

"From experience, I know what a dish will taste like before I've ever tasted it. Understanding that fats carry flavor, that salt enhances it and that acidity provides balance allows you to build more complex flavors, creating deliciousness, a mouth-watering sensation that we chefs work to achieve."

Tim McKee, chef, winner of the 2009 James Beard Award for Best Chef in the Midwest

"When I wasn't at school, I was experimenting at home, and became a bit of a Mad Scientist. I did hours of research on mayonnaise, for instance, and though no one else seemed to care about it, I thought it was utterly fascinating. . . . By the end of my research, I believe, I had written more on the subject of mayonnaise than anyone in history."

Julia Child, *My Life in France*

DASHING VINAIGRETTE

INGREDIENTS

→ 1 tablespoon (11 g) Dijon mustard (good mustard makes good vinaigrette)

→ 1 tablespoon (15 ml) vinegar (choose your favorite) or lemon juice

→ 3 tablespoons (45 ml) mild olive oil or vegetable oil

EQUIPMENT

→ Fork or wire whisk

→ Small bowl

SAFETY TIPS AND HINTS

Choose your favorite vinegar for your vinaigrette. Rice or cider vinegar tend to be milder than red or white wine vinegar. Sherry vinegar is our family's favorite.

If you prefer lemon juice, fresh-squeezed is best! Don't like mustard? Mix 1 tablespoon (15 ml) lemon juice with 3 tablespoons oil and season to taste with salt and pepper.

CHALLENGE LEVEL	TIME	YIELD
🔴	15 minutes	5 tablespoons (75 ml) dressing

CREATE THE BEST-DRESSED SALAD IN TOWN WITH THIS TANGY EMULSION.

Fig. 4: Taste the vinaigrette.

Fig. 1: Add mustard and vinegar to a small bowl.

Fig. 2: Whisk the mustard and vinegar.

Fig. 3: Stir in oil until a thick emulsion forms.

Fig. 5: Dress your favorite salad with the vinaigrette you prepared.

THE SCIENCE
BEHIND THE FOOD:

Vinaigrette is an emulsion of oil and a mild acid, such as vinegar or lemon juice. Emulsions are simply mixtures of two things that are normally immiscible (unmixable), like water and oil.

In an emulsion, a group of one type of molecule surrounds individuals or small groups of another type of molecule. Imagine chemicals playing ring-around-the-rosy with one or two people in the middle who would rather not be there, and you'll get the idea. It helps to add a mediator called a surfactant to get between the immiscible molecules and stabilize the mixture.

In this vinaigrette, the proteins in the mustard act as surfactants. The vinegar or lemon juice adds tartness to the mixture, and the salt in mustard makes it taste great!

RECIPE

1. Combine the mustard with vinegar or lemon juice in the bowl. **(Fig. 1)**

2. Whisk the mixture until well blended. **(Fig. 2)**

3. Drizzle the oil into the mustard/vinegar mixture a little bit at a time, whisking as you do.

4. Stir the mixture vigorously until a thick, shimmery emulsion forms between the oil and vinegar. **(Fig.3)**

5. Taste the salad dressing. If the vinegar is too strong for your taste, add another tablespoon of oil and taste it again. **(Fig. 4)**

6. If an emulsion won't form, let the mixture sit for a few minutes, add a few drops of warm water and try again.

7. Use the vinaigrette to dress your favorite salad, sandwich, or vegetable. **(Fig. 5)**

CREATE AND COMBINE
Try your hand at making Awesome Aioli (Lab 16), another emulsion!

Make vinaigrettes using different vinegars and oils, depending on what flavors you want to pair with a salad.

INGREDIENTS

→ 1 large egg

→ 2 teaspoons (10 ml) lemon juice

→ 1 teaspoon Dijon mustard

→ ¼ teaspoon kosher salt

→ 1 teaspoon (5 ml) cold water

→ ½ cup (120 ml) olive oil or neutral oil, such as safflower or canola

→ Hot sauce, optional, for taste

→ Garlic, optional, for taste

→ Chopped herbs, optional, for taste

EQUIPMENT

→ Glass or stainless-steel round-bottomed mixing bowl

→ Small saucepan for coddling eggs

→ Wire whisk

→ Thermometer

CHALLENGE LEVEL	ALLERGEN ALERTS	TIME	YIELD
	Eggs	30 minutes if you coddle the eggs; 10 minutes if you use raw eggs	Around ⅔ cup (150 g) aioli

Adapted from Julia Child's mayonnaise recipe.

Fig. 6: Mix with garlic, herbs, or hot sauce.

THE WORD "AIOLI" IS USED TO REFER TO A MEDITERRANEAN EMULSION OF OLIVE OIL AND GARLIC, BUT TODAY PEOPLE USE IT TO REFER TO MAYONNAISE THAT'S BEEN FLAVORED WITH ANYTHING FROM GARLIC TO SRIRACHA. IT'S FUN AND DELICIOUS TO MAKE HOMEMADE MAYO AS A BASE FOR YOUR OWN CUSTOM CONDIMENT OR DIP.

Fig. 1: Coddle the eggs.

Fig. 2: Chill briefly on ice.

Fig. 3: Mix lemon juice, mustard, and salt.

Fig. 4: Drizzle oil in as you whisk.

Fig. 5: Whisk until thick.

THE SCIENCE
BEHIND THE FOOD:

The iconic chef and cookbook author Julia Child was a self-described mad scientist and experimented extensively in her kitchen, doing hours of research on mayonnaise.

She discovered that mayonnaise emulsified best when using room-temperature ingredients, by beating the egg yolk for a minute or two before adding the oil, and by adding the oil very gradually at first. Read more about emulsions in Lab 15.

Pasteurization is a method of using heat to kill bacteria. Heating the eggs at 140°F (60°C) for 3 minutes kills bacteria that may be present, without solidifying the egg proteins.

SAFETY TIPS AND HINTS

All of the ingredients should be at room temperature before you start.

I recommend coddling the eggs (see recipe) to kill any bacteria that may be present, but mayo can be made with raw eggs as well. Coddle large eggs for 3 minutes and extra-large eggs for 5 minutes.

RECIPE

1. Coddle a few eggs. In a saucepan on the stove, bring water to 140°F (60°C) and remove it from the heat. If it's hotter than 140°F, wait for it to cool to the desired temperature. Place the eggs in the 140°F water for 3–5 minutes, depending on the size of the eggs. **(Fig. 1)** Remove them to a bowl of ice water for 3 minutes. **(Fig. 2)** Then, take the eggs out of the ice water and put them in a bowl of room-temperature water for a few more minutes.

2. Warm a mixing bowl using hot water. Dry the bowl. Crack an egg and put the yolk in the mixing bowl.

3. Whisk the egg yolk for 2 minutes.

4. Add the lemon juice, mustard, salt and 1 teaspoon cold water and whisk everything together until frothy. **(Fig. 3)**

5. Whisking constantly, slowly dribble in the oil a drop at a time until the mayonnaise starts to thicken and the oil is incorporated. **(Fig. 4)**

6. When the mayonnaise emulsifies and gets thicker, you can add the oil in a thin stream instead of drop by drop. **(Fig. 5)**

7. (Optional) Mix the mayonnaise with garlic, herbs, or your favorite hot sauce to create a dip or spread. **(Fig. 6)**

CREATE AND COMBINE
Add homemade pesto (Lab 20) to your aioli to give it a basil and garlic punch.

HEAVENLY HUMMUS

INGREDIENTS

→ 2 cups (480 g) canned chickpeas

→ 2 tablespoons (28 ml) ice-cold water, more if needed

→ 1 lemon

→ 1 clove garlic, minced

→ 1 teaspoon kosher salt

→ ½ cup (120 g) tahini (sesame seed paste)

→ Olive oil (optional)

EQUIPMENT

→ Food processor or blender

→ Juicer or citrus press

CHALLENGE LEVEL	TIME	YIELD
	20 minutes	Around 2 ½ cups (625 g) hummus

HUMMUS IS DELICIOUS ON EVERYTHING FROM PITA CHIPS TO CARROT STICKS. THIS VERSATILE HIGH-PROTEIN PURÉE ORIGINATED IN THE MIDDLE EAST AND IS QUICK AND SIMPLE TO MAKE AT HOME USING CANNED CHICKPEAS.

Adapted from *Jerusalem: A Cookbook* by Yotam Ottolenghi and Sami Tamimi.

Fig. 5: Serve hummus with veggies and pita bread or chips.

Fig 1: Juice the lemon.

Fig. 2: Add the ingredients to the blender.

food processor works best for making hummus, but a
blender will do.

Food processor blades are extremely sharp. Adult
supervision is recommended.

Fig. 3: Blend the mixture into a thick
paste.

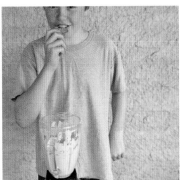

Fig. 4: Taste and adjust seasoning.

RECIPE

Juice a lemon. **(Fig. 1)**

. Add the chickpeas, garlic, lemon juice, and tahini to a food
processor or blender. **(Fig. 2)**

. Blend into a thick paste. **(Fig. 3)**

. Add the ice-cold water and blend again until the mixture is
smooth and creamy. Taste it and add salt as needed. **(Fig. 4)**

. Drizzle with olive oil (optional) and serve with pita bread,
pita chips, potato chips, or fresh vegetables. You can also
serve hummus as a main dish, or as a bed for meatballs or
lamb. **(Fig. 5)**

CREATE AND COMBINE

Make meatballs (Lab 28) using ground lamb or turkey and
Mediterranean seasoning to serve with the hummus.

THE SCIENCE BEHIND THE FOOD:

Puréed means "purified," and puréed foods such as
hummus usually consist of cooked fruits, vegetables, or
beans that have been mashed, blended, or ground up.

Puréeing food makes it easier for some people to eat,
and scientists are studying whether blending food
actually changes the way you digest it. They've found
that grinding up fiber, such as the fiber in chickpeas,
doesn't diminish its healthy effects, so keep on dipping
into that hummus.

LIP-SMACKING ALFREDO

INGREDIENTS

→ 4 tablespoons (55 g) butter

→ 1 cup (235 ml) heavy whipping cream

→ 1 cup (100 g) grated Parmesan cheese, lightly packed, plus more for thickening sauce and serving

→ Salt

→ Pepper

→ 1 clove garlic (optional)

EQUIPMENT

→ Cheese grater

→ Knife

→ Large skillet or sauté pan

→ Mixing spoon

→ Stove

SAFETY TIPS AND HINTS

Good-quality Parmesan makes the best Alfredo sauce.

If you want thinner sauce, add more cream. For a thicker sauce, throw in more Parmesan cheese.

CHALLENGE LEVEL	ALLERGEN ALERTS Dairy	TIME 15 minutes	YIELD Around 2 cups sauce

THIS EGG-FREE VERSION OF A CLASSIC RECIPE IS PERFECT FOR COATING PASTA WITH A CREAMY, RICH SAUCE THAT EVEN THE PICKIEST EATER WILL LOVE. PAIR WITH VEGETABLES AND PROTEIN TO CREATE A MOUTHWATERING MEAL.

Fig. 4: Alfredo sauce can stand on its own or be paired with other pasta toppings.

Fig. 1: Add cream to melted butter.

Fig. 2: Throw together a pasta bar.

Fig. 3: Invite your friends.

Fig. 5: You can add chicken and vegetables to make a meal.

THE SCIENCE
BEHIND THE FOOD:

Sauce becomes more viscous (thickens) when it can't move around easily.

The best ways to thicken sauces include:

- Dissolving solids in the sauce, such as cornstarch or a flour/butter mixture called a roux

- Cooling the sauce, which slows molecular movement

- Making an emulsion, which mixes the water with globules of fat

- Adding lots of pieces of things that won't dissolve completely but will interfere with movement, such as herbs or hard cheese

In this recipe, emulsified fat from the butter and cream creates a thick sauce, which will get thicker as it cools. Adding lots of Parmesan adds flavor and thickens the sauce more.

RECIPE

1. Grate the Parmesan cheese.

2. If using garlic, finely dice it.

3. Melt the butter in a large skillet. If you're using garlic, add it to the butter and cook on medium for 2 minutes. Don't allow the garlic to brown, or the sauce will have a bitter taste.

4. Add the cream to the butter and stir.

5. Add the grated Parmesan and stir over medium-low heat for a few minutes, until the sauce is smooth. **(Fig. 1)**

6. Taste the sauce. If you want it thinner, add more cream. To make it thicker, add more shredded cheese. Season to taste with salt and pepper.

7. Serve sauce plain, or add chicken and veggies. **(Fig. 2, 3, 4, 5)**

CREATE AND COMBINE

Stir-fry or steam some veggies (Lab 30) to go with the Alfredo. A salad (Lab 32) would make a super side dish.

TONY TOMATO SAUCE

INGREDIENTS

→ 5 tablespoons (70 g) butter

→ 1 (28-ounce [800 g]) can of whole, peeled tomatoes with their juices (around 2 cups)

→ 1 yellow, white, or sweet onion

→ Salt

→ Basil, for flavor

EQUIPMENT

→ Blender or hand blender (optional)

→ Knife

→ Large saucepan

→ Spoon

→ Stove

SAFETY TIPS AND HINTS

If you like tomato chunks, you can skip blending.

This sauce is good with any kind of canned tomatoes, but San Marzano are my favorite. Use whole, peeled tomatoes without added sugar or corn syrup for the best results.

CHALLENGE LEVEL	ALLERGEN ALERTS	TIME	YIELD
🍳🍳	Dairy	1 hour	Around 2 cups (490 g) sauce

WITH THIS SIMPLE TOMATO SAUCE, COOKBOOK AUTHOR MARCELLA HAZAN CREATED A PERFECT PAIRING OF ACID AND BUTTERFAT. ONE BITE WILL WIN YOUR HEART (AND YOUR TASTE BUDS).

Adapted from a recipe by Marcella Hazan.

Fig. 4: Cook the sauce uncovered.

THE SCIENCE
BEHIND THE FOOD:

Tomatoes are a member of the nightshade family, along with potatoes, eggplant, and the deadly belladonna plant. Luckily, tomatoes are perfectly safe to eat, and they contain chemical compounds that are good for you, including vitamin C and the pigment lycopene, which gives red tomatoes their brilliant color.

Besides being pretty and nutritious, tomatoes can help balance a dish by adding both acid and sweetness. The right combination of sweet, salt, bitter, sour, and umami lends balance or roundness of flavor to a dish. Add a little salt to a tomato and you have a trifecta of flavor. Throw in some butterfat and you've created a masterpiece.

RECIPE

1. Cut an onion in half, keeping the ends intact to hold it together. Remove the peel. **(Fig. 1, 2)**

2. Melt the butter in the saucepan over medium heat.

3. Add the tomatoes and halved onion to the pan, along with a pinch of salt. **(Fig. 3)**

4. Cook the sauce, uncovered, for 45 minutes or so. **(Fig. 4)**

5. Mash the tomatoes with a spoon, stir the sauce, and taste it, adding salt as needed. Remove the onion.

6. Ladle the sauce into a blender or use a hand blender to purée it (optional). **(Fig. 5)**

7. Serve the sauce over your favorite pasta and share the recipe with a friend. **(Fig. 6)**

CREATE AND COMBINE

Make homemade pasta (Lab 22) to go with your sauce or use it on pizza crust (Lab 24).

Fig. 1: Cut the onion.

Fig. 2: Remove the peel.

Fig. 3: Add tomatoes.

Fig. 5: Puree the tomatoes (optional)

Fig. 6: Serve the sauce over pasta.

NUT-FREE PESTO

INGREDIENTS

→ 4 cups (120 g) fresh basil leaves, lightly packed (or herb of your choice)

→ 1 cup (100 g) fresh Parmesan cheese (you can use dehydrated Parmesan, but freshly-grated is better!)

→ 1 cup (235 ml) olive oil

→ 1 clove fresh garlic, minced (optional)

EQUIPMENT

→ Blender or food processor

CHALLENGE LEVEL	TIME 15 minutes	YIELD Around 2 cups pesto

Fig. 5: Mix with your favorite pasta.

BURSTING WITH FLAVOR, THIS VERDANT SAUCE MADE FROM FRESH BASIL IS DELICIOUS ON EVERYTHING FROM POTATO CHIPS TO BOW-TIE PASTA. AFTER YOU TRY IT WITH BASIL, EXPERIMENT WITH YOUR FAVORITE HERBS TO CREATE A CUSTOM BLEND.

Fig. 1: Wash the basil.

THE SCIENCE
BEHIND THE FOOD:

Blending basil and garlic breaks up their cells, releasing wonderful flavors that will liven up any dish. Oil prevents the basil from coming into contact with oxygen, preserving its beautiful bright green color.

Garlic belongs to the plant genus *Allium* and is related to lilies. Members of this family contain an element called sulfur. Blending up garlic cells allows chemical scissors called enzymes to interact with other garlic chemicals, releasing the smell and flavor that most people associate with raw garlic.

Fig. 2: Add the ingredients to the blender.

Fig. 3: Use a spoon to smash the leaves down.

RECIPE

1. Wash the basil well, rinse it and pat it dry. **(Fig. 1)**

2. Add the garlic, basil, Parmesan, and oil to the blender or food processor. **(Fig. 2)**

3. Blend until smooth. You may have to stop the blender and push down on the basil with a spoon a few times. **(Fig. 3, 4)**

4. Serve pesto as a dip or use it as pizza or pasta sauce. **(Fig. 5, 6)**

5. Store refrigerated or freeze pesto in an ice cube tray to use later.

CREATE AND COMBINE

Make your own pasta (Lab 22) or pizza dough (Lab 24) to enjoy with the pesto.

Experiment with other green sauces, such as chimichurri, by blending other herbs. Choose one strong-flavored herb (such as basil, mint, or dill) and mix it with milder herbs (such as parsley or chives). You can also play with the texture of the green sauce by chopping herbs by hand.

Fig. 4: Blend until smooth.

Fig. 6: Enjoy!

BEST BEURRE BLANC

INGREDIENTS

JULIA CHILD'S SAUCE

→ ¼ cup (60 ml) white wine vinegar

→ ¼ cup (60 ml) dry white wine

→ 1 tablespoon (10 g) minced shallots (optional)

→ 2 sticks (225 g) cold butter (not clarified butter)

→ Salt

→ Pepper

WINE-FREE VERSION

→ ¼ cup (60 ml) white wine vinegar

→ ¼ cup (60 ml) heavy whipping cream

→ 1 tablespoon (10 g) minced shallots (optional)

→ 1 stick (112 g) cold butter (not clarified butter)

→ Salt

→ White pepper

OPTIONAL

→ Vegetables to roast

→ Olive oil

EQUIPMENT

→ Medium or large skillet

→ Mixing spoon

→ Stove, grill, and/or oven

→ Wire whisk

CHALLENGE LEVEL	ALLERGEN ALERTS	TIME	YIELD
👨‍🍳👨‍🍳	Dairy	10 minutes	Around 1 cup (240 g) sauce

JULIA CHILD LEARNED TO MAKE THIS CLASSIC FRENCH SAUCE AT A DINNER PARTY. IT COMBINES BUTTER, WINE, AND VINEGAR TO CREATE A DREAMY TOPPING THAT BRINGS OUT THE BEST IN VEGETABLES, CHICKEN, OR FISH.

Adapted from *Julia and Jacques Cooking at Home* by Julia Child and Jacques Pépin.

Fig. 5: Serve with fish, chicken, or sweet corn.

Fig. 1: Toss the vegetables in olive oil.

Fig. 2: Grill or roast veggies to go with your sauce.

Fig. 3: Cut the butter into smaller pieces.

Fig. 4: Reduce the wine and vinegar. Add butter.

Fig. 6: Beurre blanc is delicious with rice and vegetables too.

RECIPE

1. If you're making vegetables, toss them with some olive oil. **(Fig. 1)**

2. Grill or roast the vegetables (see Lab 30) while you make the sauce. **(Fig. 2)**

3. Cut the butter into 16 pieces. **(Fig. 3)**

4. Add the wine (if using) and vinegar to a medium or large skillet. Turn the heat up to medium high.

5. Add the shallots (if using) to the liquid.

6. Reduce the liquid by boiling it down to a syrupy glaze and remove it from the heat. **(Fig. 4)**

7. Immediately whisk in two lumps of cold butter. If you're making the wine-free version, add the cream here.

8. Set the pan back on the stove over low heat and continue to whisk in the butter a piece at a time, adding a new one each time the previous one melts.

9. When the last piece of butter has melted, turn the heat off and taste the sauce. Add salt and pepper to season.

10. Serve the sauce with fish, chicken, or sweet corn. **(Fig. 5)**

11. Buerre Blanc is delicious on vegetables and rice too. **(Fig. 6)**

CREATE AND COMBINE

Toss homemade pasta (Lab 22) with beurre blanc or drizzle it over roasted potatoes (Lab 31).

SAFETY TIPS AND HINTS

The alcohol in wine evaporates during cooking, but there is a wine-free alternative for those who prefer it.

THE SCIENCE BEHIND THE FOOD:

Emulsions are solutions of droplets suspended in a liquid they usually won't mix with. These droplets are stabilized and stay more evenly mixed when they're combined with another substance called an emulsifier.

Beurre blanc is an emulsion of butter and liquid. Milk solids in the butter serve as emulsifiers, keeping the buttery fat globules suspended in the mixture. If the sauce gets too hot and the butterfat separates from the solids, the emulsion will "break," leaving an oily mess.

Keeping the heat turned down as you add the chilled butter allows you to combine lots of butterfat into the emulsion without breaking it.

MARVELOUS MAIN DISHES

MAIN DISHES SERVE UP ALL KINDS OF SCIENCE.

Meatballs are a popular, delicious protein, and it's important to learn to cook them correctly. A simple thermometer will do the trick.

Homemade pasta and pizza dough get their fabulous texture from the wheat protein gluten, souffles and crêpes delve into egg science, and brittle rice paper makes an astonishingly flexible wrap when you get it wet.

Once you master the basics of these main courses, use your creative superpowers to give them your own signature style.

"Good cooking is all about art. Good cooking is all about science. And GREAT cooking is about both, which is why understanding our creative process and our scientific principles are key to making the best food possible. And the science is most important to young cooks because anyone can learn it. Those principles, the mechanical side to understanding food, necessarily must precede the artistic process unless you are a one-in-a-million Picasso of a chef."

Andrew Zimmern, chef, writer, traveler, and TV host

HOMEMADE PASTA

INGREDIENTS

→ 2 large eggs

→ 2 cups (250 g) all-purpose flour, plus extra for kneading, rolling, and cutting the noodles

→ 3 tablespoons (45 ml) water, plus 3 tablespoons (45 ml) more as needed

EQUIPMENT

→ Clean dish towel

→ Flat surface, such as a large wooden cutting board, for kneading dough

→ Fork

→ Knife

→ Large bowl

→ Pasta machine or rolling pin and knife

→ Stove

SAFETY TIPS AND HINTS

You can make thinner ribbons using a pasta machine. Rolling the dough out by hand gives you delicious but thicker noodles that will have to be cooked longer.

CHALLENGE LEVEL	ALLERGEN ALERTS	TIME	YIELD
	Eggs, wheat	45 minutes	Around 4 cups (560 g) cooked pasta

FEW THINGS ARE MORE REWARDING THAN CREATING RIBBONS OF FRESH PASTA TO BLANKET WITH YOUR FAVORITE SAUCE. PASTA MACHINES WORK BEST FOR ROLLING OUT THIN, UNIFORM NOODLES, BUT A ROLLING PIN AND KNIFE WILL DO THE TRICK IF YOU DON'T HAVE ONE.

Adapted from *Sunset Pasta Cook Book.*

Fig. 5: Cook the pasta in lots of boiling, salted water

Fig. 1: Make a well in the flour to mix eggs into.

Fig. 2: Mix the dough.

Fig. 3: Knead the dough.

Fig. 4: Roll the pasta into sheets and cut it into noodles.

Fig. 6: Serve pasta with some olive oil or your favorite sauce.

RECIPE

1. Add 2 cups (250 g) of flour to a large bowl in a mound.

2. Create a well in the middle of the hill of flour.

3. Break the eggs into the depression you made and mix them up well using a fork. **(Fig. 1)**

4. Stir 2 tablespoons (30 ml) of water into the egg.

5. Start mixing the flour into the egg mixture.

6. Add another 1 tablespoon (15 ml) of water and continue mixing. **(Fig. 2)**

7. When the dough gets too hard to stir with a fork, use your hands to finish mixing and create a ball of dough.

8. Add flour to a work surface and knead the dough for a few minutes. **(Fig. 3)**

9. Put the dough in a bowl and cover with plastic wrap or a damp dish towel. Let it rest for half an hour.

10. Divide the dough into fourths. Use a pasta machine or rolling pin to roll one part into a sheet. If using a machine, begin rolling using the widest setting and move to thinner ones until you achieve the desired noodle thickness.

11. Cut the pasta into strips (or leave it uncut to make lasagna noodles). **(Fig. 4)**

12. Hang the pasta over a clean dish towel on the back of a chair to keep it from sticking together.

13. Cook the pasta in salted, boiling water until tender and serve it with your favorite sauce. **(Fig. 5, 6)**

CREATE AND COMBINE

Mix up homemade tomato sauce (Lab 19) or pesto (Lab 20) to serve on the pasta you made.

Make panir (Lab 11) to layer on homemade lasagna noodles.

THE SCIENCE BEHIND THE FOOD:

Most pasta is dried for storage before it hits the market. Fresh pasta contains more water, but it also contains uncooked flour and eggs, so it must be boiled like dried pasta.

Ideally, $\frac{1}{4}$ pound (115 g) of pasta should be cooked in at least 4 cups (about 1 liter) of salted water until it is no longer rubbery but is not mushy. Perfectly cooked pasta is said to be toothy, or al dente. A wheat protein called gluten gives pasta its chewy texture.

After cooking, pasta should be drained and may be briefly rinsed with hot water to remove starch that can make it stick together.

PERFECT POPOVERS

INGREDIENTS

→ 2, room temperature, fresh eggs

→ 1 cup (235 ml) whole milk

→ 1 tablespoon (15 ml) melted butter

→ 1 cup minus 2 tablespoons (100 g) all-purpose flour

→ ½ tsp salt

→ Cooking spray, oil or butter

EQUIPMENT

→ Bowls

→ Oven

→ Popover pan or heavy muffin tin

→ Wire whisk

CHALLENGE LEVEL	ALLERGEN ALERTS	TIME	YIELD
🍳🍳🍳	Dairy, eggs, wheat	Around 2 hours total	6 large popovers or 12 small ones

Fig. 5: Serve popovers hot with butter and honey.

THESE SCRUMPTIOUS BREAD BALLOONS INFLATE WITH STEAM AS THEY BAKE AND ARE HEAVENLY WHEN SLATHERED WITH BUTTER AND HONEY, OR YOUR FAVORITE JAM.

Recipe from my friend Mary Warner.

RECIPE

1. Lightly coat a popover pan or muffin tin with the oil, butter, or cooking spray.

2. Break the eggs into a bowl. Whisk the eggs and milk together. **(Fig. 1)**

3. Stir in 1 tablespoon melted butter.

Fig. 1: Break the eggs into a bowl.

Fig. 2: Whisk the dry ingredients into the egg and milk mixture.

Fig. 3: Fill the cups about halfway full of batter.

Fig. 4: Lower the temperature and bake until golden brown.

THE SCIENCE BEHIND THE FOOD:

Popover batter is made from approximately equal parts of flour and liquid and is called a pour batter.

Flour and eggs are the elastic in the batter. When liquid and heat are added to flour, its stretchy gluten proteins and starch create a network of structure. The proteins in egg whites provide additional elasticity to the batter. Salt helps the flour absorb moisture from the milk and eggs and adds flavor to popovers.

When the pan is placed in a hot oven, the moisture in the batter vaporizes and becomes trapped inside a network of flour and egg proteins, inflating the popover like a balloon. Turning the heat down partway through the baking process allows the proteins and starches to become irreversibly set into place, creating a delicious bread with a hollow interior, perfect for filling with butter and honey.

4. Combine the flour and salt in a separate bowl, mix well, and then whisk them into the eggs and milk. **(Fig. 2)**

5. Let the mixture rest at room temperature for around 1 hour.

6. Preheat the oven to 425°F (220°C).

7. Pop the empty pan into the oven for about 5 minutes to heat the metal.

8. Fill the cups in the hot pan about halfway full of popover batter. **(Fig. 3)**

9. Bake at 425°F (220°C) for 10 minutes on the center rack of the oven.

10. Lower the oven temperature to 375°F (190°C) and continue baking until golden brown. Depending on the size of the pan, this will take another 25–35 minutes. **(Fig. 4)**

11. Remove the popovers from the pan and serve hot with butter and honey or jam. **(Fig. 5)**

CREATE AND COMBINE
Pair Popovers with homemade yogurt (Lab 13) and jam for a tasty breakfast.

PIZZA DOUGH

INGREDIENTS

→ 1 cup (235 ml) warm (not hot) water

→ 2 teaspoons yeast (or 1 teaspoon if you prefer thinner crust)

→ 3 cups all-purpose flour, plus extra for kneading

→ 1 teaspoon salt

→ 1 tablespoon (15 ml) oil, such as olive oil

EQUIPMENT

→ Baking sheet, pizza stone, or pizza-sized grilling basket

→ Flat surface, such as a large wooden cutting board, for kneading dough

→ Large bowl

→ Mixing spoon

→ Oven or grill

→ Plastic wrap or dish towel

CHALLENGE LEVEL	ALLERGEN ALERTS Wheat	TIME 1 hour	YIELD Dough for 1 large pizza or 3-4 small ones

Fig. 5: Homemade pizza.

PIZZA IS ONE FOOD THAT EVERYONE IN OUR FAMILY CAN AGREE ON. FIRE UP THE GRILL OR TURN ON THE OVEN TO CREATE MOUTHWATERING PERSONAL PIZZAS WITH CHEWY HOMEMADE CRUST.

RECIPE

1. Add 2 teaspoons yeast to 1 cup (235 ml) warm water and let it sit for 5 minutes.

2. In a large bowl, mix 3 cups flour with the salt and then stir in the oil and the yeast mixture to create dough.

3. Briefly knead the dough and then put it back in the bowl. Cover it with plastic wrap or a damp dish towel and let it rise for half an hour. **(Fig. 1)**

SAFETY TIPS AND HINTS

Add 1 teaspoon yeast instead of two for less puffy dough.

Prebake crusts for 5 minutes before adding super-soggy ingredients, like lots of fresh tomatoes or extra sauce.

THE SCIENCE
BEHIND THE FOOD:

Wheat protein is the secret to making chewy, delicious pizza crust.

When particles of wheat flour are added to water and then stirred, the proteins form a unique elastic complex called gluten. Gluten can absorb large amounts of water, and kneading allows gluten complexes to come into contact with more gluten to form superlong elastic structures.

These gluten strands make pizza chewy and are exceptional at trapping bubbles. You'll often see big bubbles in really good pizza crust.

Sugar gets in the way of gluten and is sometimes added to dough to create more tender crust.

4. Punch the dough down and preheat an oven or grill to 400°F (200°C). **(Fig. 2)**

5. Flatten and stretch the dough. **(Fig. 3)**

6. Add your toppings and bake in an oven or on a grill. **(Fig. 4)**

7. Enjoy your pizza! **(Fig. 5, 6)**

CREATE AND COMBINE

Make homemade tomato sauce (Lab 19), mozzarella (Lab 10), and/or pesto (Lab 20) to top your pizza.

Fig. 1: Knead the dough and allow it to rise.

Fig. 2: Punch down the dough and get ready to make pizza.

Fig. 3: Flatten and stretch the dough.

Fig. 4: Add toppings and bake in the oven or on the grill.

Fig. 6: Dig in!

LAB 25

SKY-HIGH SOUFFLÉ

INGREDIENTS

→ 1½ cups (355 ml) of milk (whole, 2%, or 1%)

→ 3 tablespoons (42 g) butter, plus 1 tablespoon (14 g) for greasing soufflé dish(es)

→ ⅓ cup (33 g) grated Parmesan cheese, loosely packed

→ 1 cup (120 g) Gruyère cheese, loosely packed

→ 4 tablespoons (31 g) sifted all-purpose flour

→ ½ teaspoon salt, plus extra

→ ¼ teaspoon white pepper (optional)

→ 6 egg yolks

→ 7 egg whites

→ ⅛ teaspoon cream of tartar

→ 2 tablespoons (20 g) minced shallot (optional)

EQUIPMENT

→ 2-quart soufflé dish or 4-6 ramekins

→ Electric or hand mixer

→ Medium or large bowl

→ Oven

→ Strainer set over a large bowl

→ Whisk

CHALLENGE LEVEL	ALLERGEN ALERTS Dairy, eggs	TIME About 1 hour, including baking time	YIELD 1 2-quart soufflé dish or 4-6 small soufflés in ramekins

Fig. 6: Soufflés should puff up above the edges of the dish.

SOUFFLÉS ARE ALWAYS FALLING DOWN ON TELEVISION AND IN MOVIES, BUT THIS FLUFFY FRENCH EGG DISH IS SURPRISINGLY EASY TO MAKE AND DELICIOUS TO EAT.

Adapted from the *New York Times* Cooking section.

RECIPE

1. Preheat the oven to 400°F (200°C).

2. Grease or spray the soufflé dishes and dust them with the Parmesan cheese.

3. Melt the butter over medium heat in the saucepan. If using diced shallot, add them to the butter and cook for 2-3 minutes.

4. Stir in the sifted flour and cook for around 3 minutes, until smooth. Don't let it brown.

Fig. 1: Cook béchamel to thicken

Fig. 2: Strain the sauce.

Fig. 3: Stir in the egg yolks.

Fig. 4: Fold in the egg whites and cheese.

Fig. 5: Spoon the soufflé into the dish or dishes.

5. Take the pan off the heat and whisk in the milk to make béchamel sauce.

6. Put the pan back on the stove and whisk briskly over medium heat until the mixture starts to thicken. Turn the heat down and simmer for another 5 minutes, scraping the bottom of the pan frequently so that the mixture doesn't burn. **(Fig. 1)**

7. Season the béchamel sauce by adding ½ teaspoon salt and ¼ teaspoon white pepper (if using). Strain the sauce into a large bowl. **(Fig. 2)**

SAFETY TIPS AND HINTS

Be careful not to overbeat the egg whites and to fold them into the sauce very gently so you don't destroy all of the bubbles.

Don't open the oven door while the soufflé is baking.

THE SCIENCE BEHIND THE FOOD:

Soufflés are fluffy mansions of flavor, built on simple foundations of egg, milk, and flour.

To avoid grainy lumps, flour granules must be suspended in fat, such as butter, to create what chefs call a roux before being combined with milk and cooked into béchamel sauce.

Once in the oven, heat forces air bubbles in the batter to expand, and the soufflé rises. Egg proteins are denatured (irreversibly unwound) and work with the milk and wheat proteins to support the cloud of deliciousness.

8. Beat the egg yolks into the béchamel sauce one at a time. **(Fig. 3)**

9. In a separate bowl, beat the egg whites over low speed until they foam. Add the cream of tartar and a pinch of salt to the egg whites.

10. Continue beating the egg whites until they form peaks, but not until they look dry.

11. Use a spatula to stir ¼ of the egg whites into the béchamel mixture. Stir in the remaining Parmesan and Gruyère and gently fold the remaining egg whites into the mix until well-combined. **(Fig. 4)**

12. Spoon the soufflé mix into the buttered dish(es) and set on a baking sheet. **(Fig. 5)**

13. Put the soufflé in the oven and immediately turn the heat down to 375°F (190°C).

14. Bake souffles in small ramekins for 12-15 minutes or a souffle in a 2 quart dish for 30-35 minutes, or until puffy and golden-brown.

15. Turn off the oven and let your soufflé(s) sit for 5 minutes to finish baking.

16. Remove the soufflé(s) from the oven and serve immediately. The center should be creamy and hot, but still saucy. Enjoy! **(Fig. 6)**

CREATE AND COMBINE

Give your soufflé a pop of flavor by beating ¼ cup (65 g) of pesto (Lab 20) into the egg yolks and reducing the milk by ¼ cup (60 ml).

Try substituting other cheeses, such as cheddar, for the Gruyère.

Find a recipe for dessert soufflé and give it a try.

SUPER SPRING ROLLS

INGREDIENTS

→ Vegetables like red peppers, avocado, carrots, cabbage, and cucumbers, cut up into long pieces, like matchsticks

→ Rice paper

→ Rice sticks, also called thin rice flour noodles or long rice Chinese vermicelli

→ ½ cup (120 ml) lime juice or rice vinegar

→ 2 tablespoons (26 g) sugar

→ ¼ cup (60 ml) soy sauce

→ ¼ cup (60 ml) water

→ Sliced scallions (optional)

→ Red pepper flakes (optional)

EQUIPMENT

→ Large bowl filled with warm water

→ Small mixing bowl

→ Whisk or mixing spoon

CHALLENGE LEVEL	TIME 30 minutes	YIELD As many as you want to make

SOME FOOD IS ALMOST TOO PRETTY TO EAT. SPRING ROLLS ARE A GORGEOUS, HEALTHY WAY TO LIVEN UP ANY MEAL, AND THEY'RE EASY TO PERSONALIZE WITH YOUR FAVORITE FILLINGS.

Fig. 6: Serve with dipping sauce.

SAFETY TIPS AND HINTS

Use safe knife practices when cutting raw vegetables.

Adding a protein, such as cooked shrimp, chicken, tofu, or hardboiled eggs, transforms spring rolls into a main dish. A slice of avocado gives them a creamy finish.

THE SCIENCE
BEHIND THE FOOD:

Rice paper and rice noodles are made using rice flour. Starch is a gelling agent that is brittle until combined with water.

Adding liquid transforms the starch into a flexible gel. Rice starch doesn't have much flavor, but it is somewhat transparent, which means you can see through it.

Bending clear, flexible rice paper around colorful, beautiful food creates culinary works of art that are both delicious and photo-worthy.

Fig. 1: Dip rice paper in warm water.

RECIPE

1. Make dipping sauce by combining lime juice, soy sauce, sugar, and water and stirring to dissolve the sugar. Garnish with sliced scallions and red pepper flakes if desired.

2. Submerge rice paper in warm water for 30 seconds, drain, and put on a plate. **(Fig. 1)**

3. Fill the center of the rice paper with veggies and noodles. Don't overfill.

4. Fold one side of the rice paper over the filling. **(Fig. 2)**

5. Fold one end over and then the other. **(Fig. 3, 4)**

6. Roll the spring roll up. **(Fig. 5)**

7. Serve with the dipping sauce. **(Fig. 6)**

CREATE AND COMBINE
Set up a spring roll bar at the dinner table so everyone can add their favorite fillings.

Make some meatballs (Lab 28) and rice (Lab 29) to enjoy with your spring rolls.

Fig. 2: Fill the center and fold one side over.

Fig. 3: Fold one end over.

Fig. 4: Fold the other end over.

Fig. 5: Roll up your spring roll.

OOH-LA-LA CRÊPES

INGREDIENTS

→ 2 tablespoons (28 g) butter, plus more for crêpe pan

→ 1 cup (125 g) all-purpose flour

→ ⅛ teaspoon salt

→ 1¼ (295 ml) cups milk

→ 2 eggs

EQUIPMENT

→ Crêpe pan or small nonstick skillet

→ Stove

→ Thin spatula

→ Whisk

CHALLENGE LEVEL	ALLERGEN ALERTS dairy, eggs, wheat	TIME 30 minutes (or 1 hour if you chill the batter)	YIELD 12-16 crêpes

WHETHER SAVORY OR SWEET, CRÊPES OFFER UP A WARM, DELICIOUS WRAP FOR YOUR FAVORITE FOODS. THEY'RE DELICIOUS WITH HAM AND MELTED CHEESE OR PESTO AND GARDEN-FRESH TOMATOES. THEY'RE ALSO DIVINE AS DESSERTS, ROLLED UP AND SPRINKLED WITH POWDERED SUGAR.

Adapted from *How to Cook Everything* by Mark Bittman.

Fig. 5: Ooh-la-la!

Fig. 1: Mix up the batter.

Fig. 2: Pour the batter into the hot crêpe pan and spread evenly.

Fig. 3: Sprinkle crêpes with powdered sugar, roll, and sprinkle again.

Fig. 4: Or fill them with your favorite savory toppings.

Fig. 6: Crêpes for dinner? Yes, please.

RECIPE

1. Melt the butter and allow it to cool for a few minutes.

2. Combine the flour and salt. Stir in the milk and whisk together until smooth.

3. Add the eggs and melted butter, blending well. **(Fig. 1)**

4. Refrigerate for 30 minutes (optional).

5. Place the crêpe pan or skillet on the stove over medium heat.

6. When the pan is hot, add ½ teaspoon butter and melt to coat the pan.

7. Mix the batter briefly and spoon about 1 tablespoon onto the hot pan. Rotate, swirl, and angle the pan to coat the bottom of the pan with batter. **(Fig. 2)**

8. When the batter looks dry on top (this will take around 30 seconds), loosen one edge with the spatula and flip it over with your fingers. Let it cook for 15 seconds on the other side. It should be brown, but not crispy.

9. Remove the crêpe to a plate and make another one. You may stack them on top of each other while you continue to cook.

10. Fill the crêpes with savory ingredients such as ham and cheese and brown them under the broiler or make dessert crêpes with powdered sugar or ice cream and chocolate sauce. **(Fig. 3, 4, 5, 6)**

CREATE AND COMBINE

Stir-fry or grill some veggies (Lab 40) to eat with your crêpes and whisk up some Alfredo sauce (Lab 18) or pesto (Lab 20) to top them off.

Make homemade ice cream (Lab 50) to roll up inside your crêpes, and chocolate ganache (Lab 41) to pour over the top.

THE SCIENCE BEHIND THE FOOD:

Water plays an active role in creating crêpes.

When you mix milk, eggs, and flour together, the starch in the flour absorbs water from the milk and eggs. Letting the batter rest for a while allows time for more moisture to be taken up.

Batter hitting a hot crêpe pan heats up quickly. The starch soaks up additional water as moisture evaporates from the surface of the crêpe, giving it the dry appearance that lets you know when to flip it over.

MOUTHWATERING MEATBALLS

INGREDIENTS

→ 1 pound (455 g) ground beef

→ 1 pound (455 g) ground pork

→ 1 egg

→ ½ cup (25 g) bread crumbs

→ ½ cup (120 ml) milk

→ 1 teaspoon salt

→ Pepper (or your favorite seasoning) to taste

EQUIPMENT

→ Aluminum foil (optional)

→ Baking sheet

→ Instant-read thermometer or meat thermometer

→ Large bowl

→ Oven

→ Spoon (optional)

→ Whisk

CHALLENGE LEVEL	ALLERGEN ALERTS	TIME	YIELD
	Dairy, eggs, wheat	45 minutes	Around 2 pounds (910 g)

MAKE SAVORY MEATBALLS, USING EGG AS A BINDING AGENT AND BREAD CRUMBS TO MAKE THEM MORE TENDER. KNOWING SOME FOOD SCIENCE WILL ENSURE THAT THE PEOPLE YOU COOK FOR DON'T GET SICK FROM UNINVITED BACTERIA.

Adapted from *How to Cook Everything* by Mark Bittman.

Fig. 5: Serve and enjoy.

Fig. 1: Beat an egg and add salt.

Fig. 2: Mix everything together.

Fig. 3: Roll the meat into balls and put them on a baking sheet.

Fig. 4: Cook the meatballs to 160°F (71°C), or 165°F (74°C) if they contain chicken or turkey.

THE SCIENCE
BEHIND THE FOOD:

It can be hard to know exactly how long to cook something, because heat transfer is complicated. For example, if you have two steaks and one is twice as thick as the other, it will take four times as long to cook the thicker steak. That's why it's important to test meat with a thermometer.

E. coli and most other pathogenic (disease-causing) bacteria in food can be killed using heat. Although microbes are usually found on the outside of meat, where they can be killed by grilling or searing, grinding meat mixes them all the way into the center, making them harder to kill.

To kill bacteria, ground beef, pork, and lamb should be cooked to 160°F (71°C), and ground poultry, such as chicken or turkey, which carry different bacteria, must be heated to 165°F (74°C).

SAFETY TIPS AND HINTS

Always wash your hands after handling raw meat.

Use a thermometer to make sure that the temperature in the center of beef or pork meatballs is at least 160°F (71°C) before you serve them.

Ground turkey, chicken, or lamb may be substituted for pork and beef. Chicken or turkey meatballs should reach at least 165°F (74°C).

RECIPE

1. Preheat your oven to 400°F (200°C) and cover a baking sheet with foil (if using).

2. In a large bowl, soak the bread crumbs in the milk until they're soft (around 5 minutes).

3. Add the ground meat to the bread crumbs and mix them using your hands or a spoon.

4. Beat the egg. Combine it with the salt and pepper or seasoning and then add it all to the meat mixture. **(Fig. 1)**

5. Use your hands to roll the meat mixture into balls around 1 1/2 inches (3.5 cm) in diameter (from one side of a sphere to the other). **(Fig. 2, 3)**

6. Put the meatballs on the baking sheet, spaced evenly, and put the sheet in the oven. Bake for 15 minutes.

7. Remove the meatballs from the oven and check the temperature using a thermometer inserted into the center of a meatball. When the internal temperature reaches 160°F (71°C), or 165°F (74°C) if using chicken or turkey, the meatballs are ready to eat. Depending on size, they generally take 15–30 minutes to heat to a safe temperature. **(Fig. 4)**

8. Serve the meatballs with your favorite pasta and sauce.

CREATE AND COMBINE

Serve the meatballs with your favorite pasta, pair them with rice (Lab 29), or pile them on top of potatoes (Lab 31) and veggies (Lab 30).

Try making your own pasta to pair with your meatballs (Lab 22)!

COURSE
06

SASSY SIDES

A GREAT SIDE DISH IS LIKE AN IDEAL SIDEKICK: IT COMPLEMENTS THE MAIN DISH AND MAKES IT BETTER WITHOUT OVERSHADOWING IT, AND THERE'S SCIENCE HIDING INSIDE.

TO MAKE FLUFFY RICE, IT'S HELPFUL TO UNDERSTAND WHICH STARCH MAKES IT STICKY. POTATOES SOAK UP WATER UNPREDICTABLY, SO ROASTING THEM IS A GOOD WAY TO ENSURE THEY'LL ALWAYS BE DELICIOUS.

Gorgeous, fresh vegetables are nutrient-packed treasures, best when they're used quickly. To maintain their flavor, nutrients, and color, they should be stored in a way that limits evaporation and then cooked correctly so they're not broken down completely or discolored by volatile acids.

"Let things taste the way they are."

Alice Waters, chef, author, and owner of Chez Panisse

FLUFFY RICE

INGREDIENTS

→ 1 cup (185 g) long-grain white rice

→ 1¾ cups (425 ml) water

→ ½ teaspoon salt

EQUIPMENT

→ Fork

→ Medium saucepan with lid

→ Stove

Be careful when removing the lid from cooked rice. The lid can be hot, and steam can cause burns.

Double or triple this recipe for a hungry crowd. Add 1¾ cups water for every cup of rice.

CHALLENGE LEVEL	TIME	YIELD
👨‍🍳 👨‍🍳	Around 30 minutes	Around 2 cups (315 g)

RICE COMES IN MANY SHAPES AND SIZES. DEPENDING ON WHAT KIND OF RICE YOU START WITH AND HOW YOU COOK IT, YOU CAN CONCOCT EVERYTHING FROM SUPERSTICKY SHORT-GRAIN RICE FOR SUSHI TO PERFECT, FRAGRANT BASMATI FOR CURRY. HERE'S A RECIPE FOR COOKING LONG-GRAIN RICE USING THE ABSORPTION METHOD.

Fig. 4: Stir-fried and roasted veggies go well on rice.

Fig. 1: Measure the rice.

Fig. 2: Rinse the rice with water.

Fig. 3: Fluff rice with a fork and enjoy.

Fig. 5: Try mixing up some beurre blanc (Lab 21) to make your dish even tastier.

THE SCIENCE
BEHIND THE FOOD:

The word *cereal* is derived from the name of the Roman harvest goddess Ceres. Cereals are edible seeds of different grasses. Rice, wheat, corn, oats, and barley are all cereals. Wild rice is another cereal, but it is not related to other rice.

Cereal grains can be separated into three parts: the bran, the germ, and the endosperm. Bran is full of minerals and is made up of the outermost layer of cells of the grain. You'll find three kinds of uncooked rice at the grocery store: brown rice, which contains bran; white rice, which has the bran removed; and precooked converted rice.

Rice contains the starches amylose and amylopectin. Long-grain rice, such as basmati, contains more amylose and yields fluffier, less sticky rice than shorter-grained rice, which contains more amylopectin.

RECIPE

1. Put the water and salt in a saucepan and bring it to a boil with the lid on.

2. In the meantime, rinse the rice with clean water a few times. **(Fig. 1, 2)**

3. Pour the rice into the boiling water and stir once.

4. Put the lid on the saucepan again and turn the heat down to low.

5. Simmer the rice for 18 minutes.

6. Keeping the lid on the pan, remove it from the heat and let it sit for 5 minutes.

7. Fluff the rice with a fork and enjoy! **(Fig. 3)**

8. Stir-fried vegetables are great with rice, and so is beurre blanc sauce (Lab 21). **(Fig. 4, 5)**

CREATE AND COMBINE
Pair the rice with stir-fried, roasted, or grilled veggies (Lab 30).

VIBRANT VEGGIES

INGREDIENTS

→ Vegetables of your choice

→ Olive oil (if roasting) or vegetable oil (if stir-frying)

→ Salt

EQUIPMENT

→ Cutting board

→ Fork

→ Knife for cutting vegetables

→ Scrub brush

→ Vegetable peeler (optional)

IF ROASTING

→ Mixing bowl

→ Oven or grill

→ Roasting pan or baking sheet

IF STIR-FRYING

→ Wok or large skillet with lid

→ Wooden chopstick or wooden spoon

IF BOILING

→ Pot

IF STEAMING

→ Pot with lid

→ Steaming basket

CHALLENGE LEVEL 🍳🍳

TIME
Varies (depending on how many vegetables you start with)

YIELD
Varies (cooking time depends on the vegetable and method)

WHETHER YOU ROAST VEGETABLES INTO CARAMELIZED BEAUTIES, STIR-FRY THEM, OR STEAM THEM TO TOOTHSOME PERFECTION, THEY MAKE ANY MEAL BETTER. COOKING WITH FRESH, IN-SEASON VEGETABLES WILL ALWAYS GIVE YOU THE PRETTIEST, TASTIEST RESULTS, BUT ROASTING IS A GREAT WAY TO LIVEN UP LESS-THAN-PERFECT VEGGIES.

Fig 4: Stir-fry in a wok or sauté pan.

SAFETY TIPS AND HINTS

Use caution when cutting crisp and fibrous veggies.

Adult supervision recommended for stir-frying.

These are general guidelines, not rules. For example, dense vegetables, like carrots, potatoes, cauliflower and onions work well for roasting, but you can experiment with others.

Fig. 1: Wash and prep your vegetables.

Fig. 2: Cut them into pieces of approximately the same size.

Fig. 3: Roast the veggies with olive oil until golden brown.

Fig. 5: Vegetables should be tender but firm.

RECIPE

ROASTING AND GRILLING (root vegetables, onions, cauliflower)

1. Pre-heat oven to 400°F (200°C), or turn your grill on and heat t to 400, if you have a grill thermometer. If you don't have a grill thermometer, cooking times may vary.

2. Wash and scrub the vegetables, peel as needed, and cut into chunks of similar sizes. **(Fig. 1, 2)**

3. Toss the vegetables with 1 or 2 tablespoons oil and a teaspoon salt and transfer to a roasting pan or place on the grill.

4. Roast or grill vegetables in the oven for 15 minutes and stir. If they start to get too brown, turn the heat down to 375°F (190°C). Repeat stirring every 15 minutes until they are golden brown and a fork goes in easily. **(Fig. 3)**

STIR-FRYING AND SAUTÉING (leafy green vegetables, green beans, peppers, broccoli)

1. Prepare the vegetables by washing, removing ends, and trimming them into long, thin pieces of equal size to help them cook quickly and evenly.

2. Add 1 tablespoon vegetable oil to a wok or 2 tablespoons to a flat skillet and heat on high until bubbles form around the wooden chopstick or wooden spoon when you touch it to the oil.

3. Carefully add the vegetables to the wok or skillet. Stand back, since the oil may splatter.

4. Stir the vegetables for 1–2 minutes, then turn the heat down slightly. **If stir-frying,** put the lid on the pan for another 1–2 minutes to complete cooking. **If sautéing,** skip the lid and stir until tender. **(Fig. 4)**

5. When vegetables are tender, salt and serve them. **(Fig. 5)**

BOILING AND STEAMING

1. Clean and trim your vegetables, like broccoli, green beans, or asparagus.

2. **If boiling,** add enough water to the pan to cover the veggies and add about a teaspoon of salt per quart of water. **If steaming,** add water and your steaming basket to the bottom of the pan.

3. Bring the water to a boil and add the vegetables.

4. **If boiling,** do *not* put a lid on the pan. **If steaming,** cover the pan.

5. Cook the vegetables until you can pierce them with a fork, but not too easily. You want them tender, but not mushy.

CREATE AND COMBINE

Serve your vegetables with homemade pasta (Lab 22), soufflé (Lab 25), or meatballs (Lab 28) or pile them on a salad (Lab 32).

Experiment with different cooking methods for a variety of vegetables.

THE SCIENCE BEHIND THE FOOD:

Vegetables are bursting with nutrients, and how you cook them determines whether you end up with a toothsome green bean bursting with vitamins or a mushy mess.

Sometimes, it's a compromise. Cooking vegetables covered in a small volume of water is the best way to trap nutrients, but covering broccoli while cooking traps volatile acids that give it an unpleasant flavor and destroy its brilliant green color. Cooking broccoli uncovered produces a vegetable that is slightly less nutritious but stays emerald green and tastes amazing.

LAB POSH POTATOES

INGREDIENTS

→ Potatoes (as many as you want to cook)

→ Olive oil or vegetable oil

→ Salt

→ Herbs (optional)

→ Minced garlic (optional)

EQUIPMENT

→ Fork

→ Mixing bowl

→ Oven

→ Potato peeler or scrub brush

→ Roasting pan or baking sheet

SAFETY TIPS AND HINTS

Be careful not to splatter hot oil when you stir the potatoes.

CHALLENGE LEVEL	TIME	YIELD
♣♣	30–120 minutes, depending on type and size of potatoes	Varies (depends on how many potatoes you use)

Fig. 2. Season with salt and pepper.

POTATOES COME IN ALL SHAPES, SIZES, TEXTURES, AND COLORS, AND MOST PEOPLE AGREE THAT THEY ARE UNIVERSALLY DELICIOUS. ROASTING IS A SIMPLE WAY TO BRING OUT THE BEST IN THIS STARCHY STAPLE.

RECIPE

1. Preheat the oven to 400°F (200°C).

2. Peel potatoes with thick skins, such as russets. Scrub small varieties with thin skins, such as red potatoes, until there is no dirt visible.

3. Cut potatoes into uniformly sized pieces. Small potatoes may be left whole. The smaller you cut them, the more quickly they'll bake.

4. Toss the potatoes with enough oil to coat them and a hefty pinch of salt. **(Fig. 1, 2, 3)**

5. Arrange the potatoes into a single layer on the baking pan or roasting sheet and put them in the oven.

6. After 15 minutes, remove the pan, stir the potatoes, and return them to the oven.

7. After 15 more minutes, remove the pan again check the potatoes for doneness by poking them with a fork. If you're adding herbs and garlic, stir them in with the potatoes. Return the potatoes to the oven. **(Fig. 4)**

8. Keep stirring and roasting the potatoes until they're golden brown and a fork goes into them easily.

9. Serve immediately or reheat potatoes in a 400°F (200°C) oven just before serving. Potatoes look pretty with green garnishes, such as parsley and other herbs. **(Fig. 5)**

CREATE AND COMBINE

Serve potatoes with any main dish, including meatballs (Lab 28). Mash them on your plate and drizzle them with homemade crème fraîche (Lab 12).

Roast some veggies with the potatoes (Lab 30). Be sure to cut them to approximately the same size as the potatoes, and roast them in a separate dish, if possible, since they may not bake at the same rate.

THE SCIENCE BEHIND THE FOOD:

Potatoes are roots called tubers, and they are packed full of nutrients, containing lots of vitamin C and more potassium per square inch than a banana.

Many of the nutrients in potatoes are contained in the skin, so roasting small potatoes without removing their thin skins is a good way to get a powerful punch of vitamins, minerals, and other natural compounds.

Boiling potatoes is trickier than roasting them, since the starch in potatoes absorbs water during cooking, and water absorption can vary from potato to potato.

Fig. 1: Add oil to the potatoes.

Fig. 3: Toss everything together to coat.

Fig. 4: Poke potatoes with a fork to test whether they're done.

Fig. 5: Garnish and serve.

SUPER SALADS

INGREDIENTS

→ Tender leafy greens, such as lettuce, spinach, arugula, and/or baby kale

→ Your favorite vegetables

→ Salad dressing, such as vinaigrette or olive oil, vinegar, and salt (optional)

→ Other toppings, such as cheese or bread cubes fried in oil (optional)

EQUIPMENT

→ Cutting board

→ Dish towel

→ Knife for cutting vegetables

→ Large bowl or small individual bowls or plates

→ Salad spinner (optional)

CHALLENGE LEVEL	TIME	YIELD
	15 minutes	Varies

A FRESH, CRISP SALAD MAKES THE PERFECT ACCOMPANIMENT FOR ANY MEAL, OR CAN STAND ALONE AS A MAIN DISH. TOSSING SALAD WITH YOUR FAVORITE DRESSING WILL HELP YOUR BODY ABSORB THE HEALTHY PUNCH OF VITAMINS CONTAINED IN EVERY LEAFY BITE.

Fig. 5: Serve with bread and your favorite salad dressing.

Fig. 1: Choose your favorite veggies.

Fig. 2: Seasonal produce is best if you can get it.

Fig. 3: Wash and dry the vegetables.

Fig. 4: Picky eater in the group? Leave some veggies on the side.

Fig. 6: Split small heads of lettuce for individual salads.

THE SCIENCE
BEHIND THE FOOD:

To keep vegetables crisp, it's important to store them in an environment that keeps them moist. Plants that have a lot of surface area, such as lettuce, wilt quickly when they're exposed to air, and some nutrients are lost in the process.

It's best to put greens in plastic zipper bags, squeeze out most of the air, and store them in the vegetable drawers of your refrigerator. This prevents drying and keeps them away from the coldest air. Leafy vegetables are prone to freezing because they contain lots of water.

SAFETY TIPS AND HINTS

Remember to use safe cutting technique when cutting vegetables.

When dressing a salad, start with a small amount of dressing and keep adding more, a little at a time until the lettuce is lightly coated. Put a dish of dressing on the table for people who want more.

RECIPE

1. Choose your favorite vegetables for a salad. In-season produce will be the freshest and tastiest. **(Fig. 1, 2)**

2. Wash the greens well by rinsing them and then putting them in a large bowl filled with water. **(Fig. 3)**

3. Remove the greens from the water by pulling them out, to leave any dirt or sand in the bowl.

4. Dry the greens in a salad spinner or using a clean dish towel. Arrange them in a large bowl or a salad bowl. Alternately, create individual salads on small plates.

5. Wash and cut up other vegetables into bite-size pieces. Add them to the salad or leave them on the side. **(Fig. 4)**

6. Dress the salad with your favorite dressing, make your own vinaigrette (Lab 15), or whisk together equal amounts of olive oil and vinegar, salting to taste, and mix it in with the greens and veggies. **(Fig. 5, 6)**

CREATE AND COMBINE
Pair your salad with bread sticks (Lab 6), serve it with a soufflé (Lab 25), or pile it onto a pizza crust (Lab 24) drizzled with olive oil and balsamic vinegar.

BOSSY CAKES, PERFECT PASTRIES, FABULOUS FROSTINGS AND FILLINGS

DESSERTS ARE DARLINGS OF FOOD SCIENCE, AND PICTURE-PERFECT RESULTS DEPEND ON ACCURATE MEASUREMENTS AND FOLLOWING PROPER PROCEDURE.

Angel food cakes are fortresses of sugar, protein, and air that reach fluffy perfection by clinging to the side of a pan, while the yellow cake and cupcakes in this book depend on fats to help stabilize their structure. Pie crust is a more delicate creature, containing pockets of fat trapped between layers of gluten to create a fabulously flaky pastry, and cream puffs are tender, edible shells for your favorite filling.

Since frosting is a cake's crowning glory, it should taste as good as it looks. Understanding the science of cream, buttercream, eggs, sugar, and chocolate will help you whip up out-of-this world fillings and toppings for the desserts you bake.

"Understanding how science plays a role in my everyday baking helps me understand the limits of each ingredient and how far I can push the envelope in creativity."

Michelle Gayer, James Beard-nominated pastry chef and owner of Salty Tart Bakery

PERFECT LAYER CAKE

INGREDIENTS

→ 4 cups plus 3 tablespoons (575 g) sifted cake flour

→ 1 ½ teaspoons baking soda

→ 2 teaspoons baking powder

→ 1 teaspoon salt

→ 2 sticks butter, room temperature, plus extra if using parchment

→ 2 cups (400 g) sugar

→ 3 eggs, room temperature

→ 2 additional egg yolks, room temperature

→ 2 teaspoons (10 ml) pure vanilla extract

→ 2 cups (475 ml) buttermilk, or 2 cups (475 ml) milk soured with 2 tablespoons (10 ml) lemon juice or vinegar

→ Cooking spray (if not using parchment)

EQUIPMENT

→ Two 8- or 9-inch (20 or 23 cm) round cake pans

→ Cooling rack

→ Electric mixer

→ Knife

→ Oven

→ Parchment (if not using cooking spray)

→ Toothpicks

CHALLENGE LEVEL 	ALLERGEN ALERTS Dairy, eggs, wheat	TIME Around 2 hours (20 minutes hands-on, 40 minutes baking, and 1 hour cooling)	YIELD Two 8- or 9-inch (20 or 23 cm) rounds

COMBINE BUTTERMILK AND BAKING SODA TO MAKE A GORGEOUS YELLOW LAYER CAKE THAT RISES TO ANY OCCASION. THE SECRET'S IN THE ACID.

Adapted from *Smitten Kitchen* Blog.

Fig. 6: Cut the cake and share it with friends and family.

Fig. 1: Cream the butter and sugar.

Fig. 2: Add the dry ingredients in batches.

Fig. 3: Pour the batter into the pans and bake.

Fig. 4: Take the cake out of the oven when a toothpick comes out clean.

Fig. 5: Frost your cake.

RECIPE

1. Preheat the oven to 350°F (180°C).

2. Spray cake pans with cooking spray or butter them and put buttered parchment in the bottom of the pans.

3. Sift together the flour, baking soda, baking powder, and salt.

4. Use a mixer to cream the butter and sugar together until completely combined. Add the vanilla and then the 3 eggs and 2 yolks, one at a time, mixing well after each addition. **(Fig. 1)**

5. Stir in the buttermilk and then beat it at low speed until it's mixed in. (Don't overmix.) The batter will look kind of like yogurt.

6. Add the dry ingredients to the batter in thirds, mixing after each addition. Don't overmix, but make sure that it is well blended. **(Fig. 2)**

7. Pour the mixture into the cake pans, dividing it equally and smoothing the top. Lift the pans up a few inches and drop them carefully onto your work surface to destroy large bubbles. **(Fig. 3)**

8. Put the cakes in the oven and bake for about 35–40 minutes. When they're done, they'll be golden brown, and a toothpick inserted in the center will come out clean. **(Fig. 4)**

9. Cool them for about 15 minutes on the baking rack.

10. Use a knife to loosen the edges and carefully flip the cakes over onto the cooling rack. In about 1 hour the cakes should be cool enough to frost.

11. Frost and enjoy! **(Fig. 5, 6)**

CREATE AND COMBINE

The Perfect Layer Cake is lovely when filled and frosted with chocolate ganache (Lab 41) or filled with lemon curd and frosted with lemon-curd infused whipped cream frosting (Lab 39).

THE SCIENCE BEHIND THE FOOD:

When baking soda is combined with an acid such as buttermilk, a chemical reaction occurs that produces carbon dioxide gas bubbles. These bubbles help leaven (puff up) the cake, making it look like a sponge full of tiny holes.

It's important to add the buttermilk last, because once you mix it into the batter, bubbles begin to form immediately. Baking powder contains both an acid and a base.

The acid in buttermilk makes the texture of the cake moister and more tender as well.

WICKED-GOOD CHOCOLATE CUPCAKES

INGREDIENTS

→ 1 ¾ cups (219 g) sifted all-purpose flour

→ 2 cups (400 g) sugar

→ ¾ cup (88.5 g) cocoa powder (use Dutch cocoa powder, if you can find it)

→ 1 teaspoon baking powder

→ 2 teaspoons baking soda

→ 1 teaspoon salt

→ 1 cup (235 ml) buttermilk, or 1 cup (235 ml) milk soured with 1 tablespoon (15 ml) lemon juice or vinegar

→ ½ cup (120 ml) vegetable oil

→ 1 cup (235 ml) hot coffee

→ 1 teaspoon (5 ml) pure vanilla extract

→ Butter or cooking spray

→ 2 large or extra-large room-temperature eggs

EQUIPMENT

→ 2 cupcake pans

→ Baking rack

→ Electric mixer or hand mixer and large bowl

→ Ladle or cup

→ Medium bowl

→ Oven

→ Paper baking cups

→ Sieve or sifter

→ Spatula (optional)

→ Toothpicks

CHALLENGE LEVEL	ALLERGEN ALERTS	TIME	YIELD
♟♟♟	Dairy, eggs, wheat	1 hour	Around 2 dozen cupcakes

YOU CAN'T TASTE THE COFFEE IN THESE BEAUTIES, BUT IT TAKES THE CHOCOLATE FLAVOR TO ANOTHER LEVEL, MAKING THESE MINI CAKES A PERFECT BASE FOR ANY FROSTING OR GLAZE.

Adapted from Ina Garten's *Barefoot Contessa at Home.*

Fig. 4. Bake and cool the cupcakes.

RECIPE

1. Preheat the oven to 350°F (180°C).

2. Spray cupcake pans with cooking spray or grease them with butter. Insert the paper baking cups.

3. Sift the dry ingredients together into a mixing bowl and combine. **(Fig. 1)**

SAFETY TIPS AND HINTS

Use caution when adding the hot coffee. Make sure the mixer is on low.

These cupcakes are very moist, which makes them delicious but tricky to frost. I recommend either chilling them in the freezer for half an hour before frosting or piping the frosting on instead of spreading it.

THE SCIENCE BEHIND THE FOOD:

Taste and smell are complicated. Various flavors trigger different neural networks in our brains, and flavor enhancers can trick our sense of taste. For example, sprinkling salt on chocolate or watermelon enhances sweetness.

Chocolate and coffee have a number of overlapping flavors. Combining a little bit of coffee with chocolate makes the chocolate taste more chocolaty, and coffee tastes even better with a piece of good chocolate. Mocha anyone?

4. Add the eggs, buttermilk, oil, and vanilla to a second bowl. With the mixer on low speed, add the wet ingredients to the dry ones. **(Fig. 2)**

5. Add the coffee and mix just long enough to combine the ingredients.

6. Scrape the bowl to make sure that everything is mixed well and use a ladle or cup to fill the baking cups about ¾ of the way full. **(Fig. 3)**

7. Bake the cupcakes for 18–26 minutes, until a toothpick inserted in the center comes out clean. Cool them on a baking rack for at least 1 hour before frosting. **(Fig. 4)**

8. Sprinkle the cupcakes with powdered sugar, pipe frosting on, or freeze them for 30 minutes and frost them with a knife. **(Fig. 5)**

Fig. 1: Sift and measure the ingredients. *Fig. 2: Combine wet and dry ingredients.*

Fig. 3: Pour batter into the baking cups. *Fig. 5: Add your favorite frosting.*

HEAVENLY ANGEL FOOD CAKE

INGREDIENTS

→ 1 cup (135 g) cake flour

→ 1½ cups (300 g) sugar, divided

→ 12 egg whites (around 1½ cups, or 355 ml)

→ ½ teaspoon salt

→ 1½ teaspoons cream of tartar

→ 1½ (7.5 ml) teaspoons vanilla extract

EQUIPMENT

→ 10-inch tube pan (angel food cake pan) or ungreased loaf pan

→ Cooling rack or bottle

→ Electric mixer or hand mixer and large bowl

→ Oven

→ Serrated knife

→ Spatula

CHALLENGE LEVEL	ALLERGEN ALERTS	TIME	YIELD
🎩🎩🎩	Eggs, wheat	1 hour to mix and bake, plus 1 hour to cool	One standard-sized angel food cake

ANGEL FOOD CAKE IS DESERVING OF ITS NAME. COUNTLESS AIR BUBBLES MAKE IT LIGHT AND FLUFFY, AND EGG-WHITE PROTEINS MAKE IT STRONG ENOUGH TO CARRY LAYERS OF YOUR FAVORITE FROSTING OR FILLING.

Adapted from the *Better Homes and Gardens Cook Book.*

Fig. 9: Top with berries.

Fig. 1: Sift the flour and sugar together.

Fig. 2: Separate eggs.

Fig. 3: Fold the remaining dry ingredients into the egg whites.

RECIPE

1. Sift and measure the flour. Add ¾ cup (150 g) of the sugar. Sift together twice and set aside. **(Fig. 1)**

2. Separate the eggs and beat the egg whites. When they start to foam, add the cream of tartar, salt, and vanilla. Continue to beat them until they form soft peaks and look moist and glossy. **(Fig. 2)**

3. Immediately add the remaining ¾ cup (150 g) sugar to the egg whites and continue to beat until they form stiff peaks, but still look glossy and not dry. Do not overbeat them.

4. Sift ¼ of the flour/sugar mix into the egg whites. Fold the mixture in using a spatula, folding down the sides of the bowl and up through the center. **(Fig. 3)**

5. Gently fold in the remaining dry ingredients by fourths until just mixed. Try not to overmix.

6. Bake the cake in an ungreased tube pan or loaf pan for 35-40 minutes, until golden brown.

LAB 35

HEAVENLY ANGEL FOOD CAKE (CONTINUED)

Fig. 4: Cool the cake upside down.

Fig. 5: Cut the cake into layers.

Fig. 6: Fill between the layers.

Fig. 7: Be creative.

Fig. 10: Share your cake with a friend.

7. Invert the cake on a bottle or a cooling rack and cool for 1 hour. **(Fig. 4)**

8. Remove the cake from the pan by cutting around the edges using a serrated knife and a sawing motion. Be patient, since it will be stuck to the sides and bottom of the pan.

Fig. 8: Add sprinkles and candles.

Angel food cake is sometimes called a foam cake, since it's created by whipping up a foam of egg whites surrounded by sugar and flour. It could also be called a meringue cake, since you create a meringue (Lab 48) base to combine with flour.

Egg proteins are exceptionally good at forming air bubbles when you whip them. They also supply water that turns to steam in a hot oven and helps the cake puff up even more. Cream of tartar creates an acidic environment that not only stabilizes bubbles but acts on pigments in the flour to keep the cake white.

The cake batter sticks to the side of the pan as it rises, holding the structure in place until the egg whites are baked into a stable foam.

SAFETY TIPS AND HINTS

Keep egg yolk out of your egg whites. Fat from yolks deflates this delicate cake.

Make sure that the cake or loaf pan you use is washed well and completely grease free. Angel food cakes must cling to the pan as they bake.

Don't overbeat the egg whites, or they'll separate, and you'll end up with a disappointingly flat cake. Beat them just until soft peaks form and they look glossy.

9. For layers, slice the cake horizontally. Add your favorite filling and frost the outside. **(Fig. 5, 6, 7)**

10. Don't forget the sprinkles. **(Fig. 8)**

11. Or top with fresh berries. **(Fig. 9)**

12. Share your cake with a friend. **(Fig. 10)**

CREATE AND COMBINE
Fill your cake with lemon curd (Lab 44) and frost it with whipped cream frosting (Lab 39).

TIE-DYE ROLL CAKE

INGREDIENTS

→ 3 eggs

→ 1 cup (200 g) sugar

→ 1 teaspoon (5 ml) pure vanilla extract

→ $\frac{1}{3}$ cup (80 ml) water

→ $\frac{3}{4}$ cup (84 g) all-purpose flour

→ 1 teaspoon baking powder

→ $\frac{1}{4}$ teaspoon salt

→ Powdered (confectioners') sugar

→ Food coloring

→ Cooking spray, butter, or shortening (note: for dairy-free cake, don't use butter)

EQUIPMENT

→ 10×15×1-inch (25×38×2.5 cm) rimmed baking sheet

→ Electric mixer (stand or hand mixer)

→ Large cotton dish towel

→ Knife

→ Mixing bowl

→ Oven

→ Parchment paper or waxed paper

→ Scissors

→ Small bowls for batter

→ Spatula (optional)

→ Toothpicks

CHALLENGE LEVEL	ALLERGEN ALERTS	TIME	YIELD
🍳🍳🍳	Eggs, wheat	1 hour, not including cooling and frosting	One 10-inch-wide (25 cm) roll cake

Fig. 9: The cake is ready to frost!

THE SECRET OF THIS COLORFUL, FLEXIBLE CAKE IS IN THE SPONGE ROLL IT UP WITH WHIPPED CREAM FROSTING TO CREATE BRIGHT PINWHEELS OF DELICIOUSNESS.

Adapted from the *Better Homes and Gardens Cook Book* my mom and dad gave me when I was 11.

Fig. 1: Beat the eggs until they're thick, fluffy, and pale yellow.

Fig. 2: Fold in the dry ingredients.

Fig. 3: Add food coloring to the batter.

SAFETY TIPS AND HINTS

Suggested fillings: whipped cream frosting (Lab 39) or lemon curd (Lab 44).

Suggested frosting: whipped cream frosting (Lab 39) or buttercream frosting (Lab 40).

RECIPE

1. Preheat the oven to 375°F (190°C).

2. Lay out small bowls for the finished batter, one for each color you want in the cake.

3. Cut the parchment paper or waxed paper to fit the bottom of the baking pan. Position the paper in the bottom of the pan and spray or grease the paper and the sides of the pan.

4. Mix or sift the flour, baking powder, and salt together in a bowl and set them aside.

5. Break the eggs into a medium-sized mixing bowl and beat them on high speed until they become thick, fluffy, and pale yellow (around 5 minutes). **(Fig. 1)**

6. Beat the granulated sugar into the eggs a little bit at a time.

7. With the mixer on low speed, add the water and vanilla.

8. Using a large spoon or spatula, gently fold half of the premixed dry ingredients (Step 4) into the egg mixture. Fold in the rest of the dry ingredients until the batter is smooth. Do not overstir. **(Fig. 2)**

9. Immediately divide the batter into the small bowls you prepared. Add food coloring to each bowl and mix gently with a spoon. Overstirring will deflate the batter. **(Fig. 3)**

10. Pour one bowl of batter into the center of the pan.

11. Pour the next bowl into the center of the pan, in the middle of the first layer of batter. Repeat until all of the batter is in the pan, forming a bullseye pattern. Gently tilt the pan to spread the batter into all of the corners, if possible. **(Fig. 4)**

12. Immediately put the pan into the preheated oven and bake for 11–15 minutes, depending on the size of the pan. A toothpick inserted into the center of the cake should come out clean when it is done.

13. While the cake is baking, lay a dish towel on a flat surface and sprinkle it generously with powdered sugar. **(Fig. 5)**

Fig. 4: Add the batter to the pan, one color at a time.

Fig. 5: Sprinkle a dish towel with powdered sugar.

Fig. 6: Dust the cake with more sugar.

Fig. 7: Roll the cake up, beginning at the short end.

Fig. 8: Spread the cake with filling or frosting and roll it up again.

14. Remove the cake from the oven and loosen the sides from the pan with a knife.

15. Quickly and carefully, flip the cake over onto the sugar-coated towel.

Fig. 10: Use your imagination and some sugar to decorate the roll cake.

THE SCIENCE BEHIND THE FOOD:

A roll cake is the gymnast of the cake family.

Eggs are the backbone of this recipe. Not only do they provide structure for the cake once it reaches a certain temperature, they're wonderful at trapping pockets of air when you whip them. Adding sugar to the eggs stabilizes the air pockets and tenderizes the cake.

Most sponge cakes depend on egg whites for bubbles, but this one has an extra ingredient. Baking powder, a mix of sodium bicarbonate (baking soda) and a mild acid, creates a chemical reaction that makes carbon dioxide gas, contributing more bubbles to the mix.

Proteins and starch in flour form additional scaffolding for the bubbles, but the high sugar and low flour content of the batter creates a flexible sheet of cake that can be trained to roll without cracking.

16. Trim off any crispy parts, dust with a little more powdered sugar, and then roll the cake up in the towel, beginning at one of the short ends. Let it cool completely on a cooling rack, if you have one. **(Fig. 6, 7)**

17. Unroll the cake, spread filling or frosting on it and roll it up again—this time not rolling up the towel with it. **(Fig. 8)**

18. The roll cake is ready to dust with powdered sugar or frost. **(Fig. 9)**

19. Decorate your tie-dye masterpiece. **(Fig. 10)**

CREATE AND COMBINE

Make meringue mushrooms (Lab 48) or fondant (Lab 46) to decorate your cake.

MOM'S PIE CRUST

INGREDIENTS

→ 1½ cups (188 g) all-purpose flour, plus extra for rolling

→ ½ teaspoon salt

→ ½ cup (100 g) solid vegetable shortening (or butter, but see Tips)

→ ¼ cup (60 ml) cold water

→ **BERRY PIE FILLING** (optional)
3-4 cups (425–580 g) fresh fruit, cleaned and cut into pieces, plus fruit preserves such as strawberry jelly

→ **PEACH PIE FILLING** (optional)
peaches, ½ cup (100 g) white sugar, ¼ cup (37.5 g) brown sugar, 1 tablespoon (15 ml) lemon juice, 2 tablespoons (15 g) flour, 2 tablespoons (28 g) butter

EQUIPMENT

→ Mixing spoon

→ Oven

→ Parchment paper (optional)

→ Pastry cutter or knife and fork

→ Pastry cloth or clean dish towel

→ Rolling pin

→ Sifter or sieve (optional)

→ Whisk (optional)

→ Pie tin or pie plate

CHALLENGE LEVEL	ALLERGEN ALERTS	TIME	YIELD
	Eggs, wheat	15 minutes hands-on, plus 15–45 minutes baking time	2 crusts

Fig. 8: Take your pie to a picnic.

A ROLLING PIN IS THE ONLY TOOL YOU NEED TO WHIP UP STELLAR CRUST FOR SWEET AND SAVORY PIES. MY MOM HAS ALWAYS USED THIS RECIPE, AND IT'S HARD TO TOP. THE SECRET'S IN THE SHORTENING.

Fig. 1: Cut the shortening into the flour.

Fig. 2: Put the dough on the pastry cloth.

Fig. 3: Roll out the crusts.

SAFETY TIPS AND HINTS

Prebake crusts to fill with cooked filling, such as pudding, chocolate mousse, or fruit. Add filling before baking custard pies (such as pumpkin) or double-crust fruit pies.

You may use butter instead of vegetable shortening, but it will produce less flaky crust.

RECIPE

1. Preheat oven to 350°F (180°C).

2. Combine the flour and salt. Sift them together for perfect distribution like a pastry chef would or mix them well using a fork or wire whisk.

3. Use a pastry cutter or fork and knife to combine the flour and salt with the vegetable shortening until the shortening forms small pieces and resembles cornmeal. **(Fig. 1)**

4. Add the cold water to the flour/shortening mix and stir quickly in large circles to evenly distribute the water so that it is absorbed evenly by the dough. Do not overstir. The crust will not hold together at this point.

5. Dump the dough out onto a lightly floured cotton dish towel or pastry cloth and use the cloth to gather it into a ball. Put it on a floured surface and fold it over a few times, but don't overwork it. **(Fig. 2)**

6. Divide the dough into two balls and put one of them onto a flat surface to roll out. For extra tender dough, put it on a large piece of parchment paper to roll so that you don't have to add extra flour.

7. Flatten the dough with your hand and then use a rolling pin to roll it into a circle, from the center out, lifting up as you approach the outer edges of the circle. **(Fig. 3)**

8. When the crust is the right size, roll it onto your rolling pin to transfer it onto a pie tin. Unroll it and pinch the edges with your finger. Use excess dough to patch holes or fill in edges. **(Fig. 4, 5)**

9. Repeat steps 6–8 with the second dough ball. Use a fork to poke holes in both doughs so that steam can escape as they bake.

Fig. 4: Use the rolling pin to roll the crust onto the pie tin.

Fig. 5: Crimp the crust by pinching.

Fig. 6: Fill the baked crust.

Fig. 7: It's fun to decorate the crust.

Fig. 9: Enjoy your pie on it's own or a la mode.

10. Pre-bake the crusts or fill them and bake.

11. For a single-crust prebaked pie, bake at 350°F (180°C) until golden brown all over. If the edges start to get too dark but the center still needs to be baked more, cover them with foil until the crust is done. For fresh berry filling, melt the fruit preserves and combine them with the fresh fruit. Use the mixture to fill a single prebaked pie crust. **(Fig. 6)**

Fig. 10: Everyone loves pie.

THE SCIENCE
BEHIND THE FOOD:

Good pastry crust should be both tender and flaky.

Flakes form during baking, when rolled-out layers of protein complexes formed by wet wheat flour (gluten) create steam-filled blisters.

To keep crust tender, it's essential to control gluten development by keeping some of the flour away from water. Fats such as vegetable shortening make great waterproofing material, so it's important to do a good job of combining the fat and flour before you add water.

Some fats, such as butter and margarine, contain water, so many pastry chefs stick with pure fats such as lard or vegetable shortening to make flaky, tender crust. Others don't care for the taste of shortening and stick with butter.

12. For a double-crust pie, add the filling to an unbaked crust, poke holes in the top, and use excess crust to make decorations. Bake the for recommended time, based on the filling. For peach pie (not dairy free), mix all the ingredients together except the butter. Fill the pie and dot with the butter before adding the second crust. Bake at 400°F (200°C) for 45–50 minutes. **(Fig. 7)**

13. Everyone loves pie! Take it to a picnic or enjoy it at home. **(Fig. 8, 9, 10)**

CREATE AND COMBINE
Make pudding (Lab 43) or lemon curd (Lab 44) to fill your prebaked single-crust pie. Top with berries or whipped cream (Lab 39) or homemade ice cream (Lab 50).

CELESTIAL CREAM PUFFS

INGREDIENTS

→ 1 cup (235 ml) water

→ ½ cup (112 g) butter

→ 1 cup (125 g) sifted all-purpose flour

→ ¼ teaspoon salt

→ 4 large eggs

EQUIPMENT

→ Baking sheet

→ Cooling rack

→ Oven

→ Serrated knife

→ Saucepan

→ Stove

→ Whisk

SAFETY TIPS AND HINTS

When the water boils, melt the butter and add the flour right away. If too much water evaporates, there won't be enough moisture to expand your cream puffs to their maximum height.

CHALLENGE LEVEL	ALLERGEN ALERTS Dairy, eggs, wheat	TIME 1 hour	YIELD 10 large cream puffs

ALSO CALLED PROFITEROLES AND CHOUX A LA CRÈME, CREAM PUFFS ARE SMALLER, MORE TENDER RELATIVES OF POPOVERS. FILL THEM WITH WHIPPED CREAM OR ICE CREAM AND DUST THEM WITH POWDERED SUGAR FOR AN IRRESISTIBLE TREAT.

Adapted from the *Better Homes and Gardens New Cook Book* (1976 edition).

Fig. 4: Split and cool the cream puffs. Fill with cream.

Fig. 1: Sift ingredients together.

Fig. 2: Stir the eggs into the cooked mixture.

Fig. 3: Spoon batter onto the baking sheet.

Fig. 5: Or fill with a frozen treat.

THE SCIENCE
BEHIND THE FOOD:

Cream puff batter is almost identical to popover batter, but it contains eight times as much fat, making cream puffs more tender and rich than their much larger cousins. To compensate for the extra fat, cream puffs need more eggs than popovers to keep them structurally sound.

RECIPE

1. Preheat the oven to 400°F (200°C).

2. Grease the baking sheet using the butter or cooking spray.

3. Sift the flour and salt together. **(Fig. 1)**

4. Bring the water to a boil in the saucepan. Immediately add ½ cup butter.

5. When the butter has melted, add the sifted flour and stir until the mixture forms a cohesive ball.

6. Take the pan off the heat and let the mixture cool slightly, for about 5 minutes.

7. Add the eggs, one at a time, beating after each addition until the batter is smooth. **(Fig. 2)**

8. Use a tablespoon to drop batter onto the greased baking sheet, around 3 inches (7.5 cm) apart. **(Fig. 3)**

9. Bake at 400°F (200°C) for around 30 minutes, until the cream puffs are puffed up and golden brown.

10. Take them out of the oven, split them horizontally with the serrated knife, and cool them on a rack. **(Fig. 4)**

11. When the cream puffs are cool, fill them with your favorite ice cream, sorbet, or whipped cream. **(Fig. 5)**

CREATE AND COMBINE
You can fill cream puffs with homemade sorbet (Lab 52), ice cream (Lab 50), or lemon curd (Lab 44), It's hard to beat traditional whipped cream, though (Lab 39).

WHIPPED CREAM AND WHIPPED CREAM FROSTING

INGREDIENTS

→ 1 pint (473 ml) heavy whipping cream, well chilled

→ Powdered (confectioners') sugar, 1 cup (120 g) for frosting or 2 tablespoons for whipped cream

→ 1 teaspoon pure vanilla extract

→ ¼ teaspoon salt

EQUIPMENT

→ Chilled mixing bowl (put in the freezer for a few minutes or fill with ice water to chill)

→ Sieve or sifter

→ Small bowl

→ Stand mixer or hand mixer

SAFETY TIPS AND HINTS

Don't overbeat the cream or you'll end up with butter!

CHALLENGE LEVEL	ALLERGEN ALERTS Dairy	TIME 15 minutes	YIELD Around 4 cups whipped cream or whipped cream frosting

Fig. 5: Add some color to your creation.

WHIPPING AIR AND SUGAR INTO CREAM CREATES A FROTHY, SWEET TREAT THAT PUTS ARTIFICIAL WHIPPED TOPPINGS TO SHAME. FORTIFY WHIPPED CREAM WITH EXTRA POWDERED SUGAR AND YOU HAVE A LOVELY, LIGHT FROSTING THAT WILL COMPLEMENT ALMOST ANY CAKE.

THE SCIENCE
BEHIND THE FOOD:

Whipped cream has fat to thank for its stable foamy structure. Globules of butterfat in the cream surround bubbles of whipped-in air, like kids playing ring-around-the-rosy.

As you beat whipping cream, the bubbles form a network, stiffening the foam. If you beat the cream too long, however, the entire network can collapse, separating the butterfat from the milk.

Chilling the cream helps some of the fat crystallize, which contributes to structure, and sugar strengthens the bubbles. However, adding sugar too early can keep fat from clumping, slowing bubble formation.

Fig. 1: Add cream to the chilled bowl.

Fig. 2: Hand mixers work well for whipped cream.

Fig. 3: Beat the cream until soft peaks form.

Fig. 4: Whipped cream should stick to the beaters.

RECIPE

1. Sift the powdered sugar and salt together in the small bowl.

2. Pour the heavy whipping cream into the chilled bowl and beat until the cream looks frothy. **(Fig. 1, 2)**

3. Continue to beat the cream, adding the sugar a little at a time (2 tablespoons for whipped cream, 1 cup for whipped cream frosting).

4. Add the vanilla and keep beating. For whipped cream, stop when it holds soft peaks. For frosting, you may want to beat the cream until it forms firm peaks. It should stick to the beaters. **(Fig. 3, 4)**

5. Use the whipped cream as a topping or the whipped cream frosting to ice a cake. You can also use it to fill cream puffs. **(Fig. 5)**

6. Enjoy!

CREATE AND COMBINE

Use whipped cream to fill cream puffs (Lab 38) or top ice cream (Lab 50). Whipped cream frosting is perfect for filling and frosting a tie-dye roll cake (Lab 36) or an angel food cake (Lab 35).

JAN'S BUTTERCREAM FROSTING

INGREDIENTS

- → 5 tablespoons butter, softened but not melted
- → 1 pound (455 g) powdered (confectioners') sugar
- → Half-and-half
- → 1 teaspoon (5 ml) pure vanilla or lemon extract (optional)

EQUIPMENT

- → Stand mixer or hand mixer and bowl

SAFETY TIPS AND HINTS

This frosting can be thinned or thickened by the addition of half-and-half or powdered sugar.

CHALLENGE LEVEL	ALLERGEN ALERTS	TIME	YIELD
♟♟	Dairy	15 minutes	Around 3 cups

MY MOTHER-IN-LAW'S SIMPLE BUTTERCREAM IS OUR FAMILY'S MOST IN-DEMAND FROSTING. SHE WHIPS IT UP FOR JULY BIRTHDAYS EVERY SUMMER, AND RIOTS ENSUE IF A CAKE IS TOPPED WITH ANYTHING ELSE.

Recipe from Jan Heinecke.

Fig. 5: Enjoy the treat!

Fig. 1: Cream the butter and add sugar.

Fig. 2: Add half-and-half.

Fig. 3: Taste the frosting.

Fig. 4: Add sprinkles.

THE SCIENCE
BEHIND THE FOOD:

Butter is the base of this delicious frosting.

When cream is whipped to make butter, membranes around the butterfat are disturbed, and fat globules start to stick together. The longer cream is whipped, the more globules stick together. Eventually the butterfat separates out, leaving two phases: butterfat and liquid.

The butterfat is removed, washed, and salted but still contains some water. In the end, butter is at least 80 percent fat, which makes treats such as buttercream frosting calorie rich, but well worth a bite now and then.

RECIPE

1. Cream the butter by mixing it into a smooth paste.

2. Add the powdered sugar, a little at a time, until completely blended. **(Fig. 1)**

3. Add the vanilla or lemon extract, if using.

4. Add the half-and-half 1 tablespoon (15 ml) at a time until you reach the desired consistency. **(Fig. 2)**

5. Take the frosting and use it to frost a cake or some graham crackers. Enjoy! **(Fig. 3, 4, 5)**

CREATE AND COMBINE

Buttercream frosting is delicious on chocolate cupcakes (Lab 34) and makes a perfect base for mirror glaze (Lab 42). It's also wonderful on yellow layer cake (Lab 33) or angel food cake (Lab 35).

GORGEOUS GANACHE

INGREDIENTS

→ 4 cups (946 ml) heavy whipping cream

→ 24 ounces (4 cups) good quality chopped semisweet chocolate or high-quality semisweet chocolate chips

→ 1 teaspoon (5 ml) light corn syrup

→ 1 teaspoon (5 ml) pure vanilla extract (optional)

EQUIPMENT

→ Medium saucepan with heavy bottom

→ Mixing spoon

→ Stove

SAFETY TIPS AND HINTS

Ganache is best when made with good-quality semisweet chocolate or chocolate chips and heavy whipping cream. If the chocolate you're using has too much butterfat and the frosting looks oily, you may have to switch to lighter whipping cream.

CHALLENGE LEVEL	ALLERGEN ALERTS Dairy	TIME 30 minutes, plus cooling time	YIELD Around 6 cups (1.4 L)

Fig. 6: Make the ganache smooth or textured.

WHEN I WAS A KID, MY MOM MADE CHOCOLATE GANACHE EVERY TIME OUR FAMILY MADE ICE CREAM. WE CALLED IT HOMEMADE HOT FUDGE SAUCE AND LICKED EVERY DROP FROM OUR BOWLS. THIS CLASSIC CHOCOLATE CREAM EMULSION DOUBLES AS VELVETY FROSTING AND IS QUICK AND SIMPLE TO WHIP UP.

RECIPE

1. Pour the heavy whipping cream into a saucepan and warm over low heat. **(Fig. 1)**

2. Pour in the chocolate or chocolate chips. **(Fig. 2)**

3. Keeping the heat on low, combine the mixture until it is smooth and thick, stirring the entire time so that the chocolate doesn't burn. It will take 15–20 minutes.

4. Remove the pan from the heat and stir in the vanilla, if desired.

5. Stir in the corn syrup to help prevent crystallization.

6. Serve the ganache hot over ice cream to make sundaes or cover the surface with plastic wrap and cool it in the refrigerator to make frosting. **(Fig. 4)**

7. If cooling, stir every 15 minutes until it reaches the perfect consistency. **(Fig. 5, 6)**

8. Frosting may be stored at room temperature for 2 days or refrigerated. It will solidify in the fridge, but you can let it sit at room temperature to soften and use later.

CREATE AND COMBINE

Frost a yellow layer cake (Lab 33) with ganache frosting and you'll have a masterpiece on your hands.

It's hard to beat ice cream with warm chocolate ganache, especially when you make your own (Lab 50). Whisk in a little more warm cream if you prefer thinner chocolate.

Fig. 1: Measure the cream.

Fig. 2: Add the chocolate to the pan.

Fig. 4: Cool the ganache.

Fig. 3: Add vanilla.

Fig. 5: Frost a cake or cupcake.

THE SCIENCE BEHIND THE FOOD:

Ganache is made of solids suspended in cream and chocolate, combined with emulsified butterfat, all hanging around in a sugary syrup.

A greater ratio of cream to chocolate creates a liquid ganache, while less cream yields thicker ganache.

With semisweet chocolate, a one-to-one ratio of cream to chocolate yields a perfect cake frosting. Corn syrup acts as an interfering agent, preventing sugar crystal formation and keeping the frosting shiny.

INGREDIENTS

→ Water

→ 1 cup chopped white baking chocolate containing cocoa butter (around 6 ounces, or 175 g)

→ 1 package (2.5 teaspoons [7g]) gelatin

→ 1 cup (200 g) sugar

→ ⅓ cup (80 ml) corn syrup

→ ⅓ cup (80 ml) water

→ ½ cup (80 ml) condensed milk

→ Food coloring, as desired

Frozen cake, cupcakes, cookies, or mousse to be glazed

EQUIPMENT

→ Baking sheet

→ Hand blender (immersion blender)

→ Instant-read thermometer

→ Saucepan with heavy bottom

→ Small bowls

→ Stove

CHALLENGE LEVEL	ALLERGEN ALERTS	TIME	YIELD
🍫🍫🍫	Dairy	30 minutes, plus cooling	Around 2 cups

Fig. 6: Can you see your reflection in the glaze?

THE SECRET TO A SHINY GLAZE IS IN THE TEMPERATURE. DRIZZLE THIS DAZZLING REFLECTIVE FROSTING ONTO CAKES, CUPCAKES, COOKIES, OR FROZEN CHOCOLATE MOUSSE.

RECIPE

1. Add gelatin to 3 tablespoons (45 ml) water and let it sit for 5 minutes or more. **(Fig. 1)**

2. Bring the sugar, corn syrup, and water to a boil. (Adult supervision required.)

3. When the sugar, corn syrup, and water form a clear syrup, remove them from the heat and stir in the gelatin.

Fig. 1: Add the gelatin to water.

Fig. 2: Blend the chocolate into the gelatin solution.

Fig. 3: Cool and add food coloring.

Fig. 4: Pour over frozen pre-frosted cupcakes, cake, or mousse.

Fig. 5: You can drizzle on details.

SAFETY TIPS AND HINTS

Adult supervision is required for boiling the sugar and corn syrup mixture.

Cake, cupcakes, and cookies should be coated with frosting and frozen before pouring mirror glaze.

Mousse can be frozen in silicone pans and set on top of a small container for glazing.

Put a baking sheet under whatever you glaze, or you'll have a mess on your hands.

4. Once the gelatin is dissolved, add the white chocolate, stir, and let the mixture sit for 1 minute. **(Fig. 2)**

5. Stir in ½ cup condensed milk and blend the mixture until you have a smooth, shiny mirror glaze.

6. Divide the mixture into three or four small bowls and use food coloring to create the mirror glaze palette you desire. **(Fig. 3)**

7. Check the temperature in each bowl. When they have cooled to 95°F (35°C), remove the desserts you want to glaze from the freezer and set them on small bowls or upside-down muffin tins centered over a baking sheet.

8. Pour the mirror glaze over the desserts, coating them well. Use a different color to drizzle design. **(Fig. 4, 5)**

THE SCIENCE BEHIND THE FOOD:

When gelatin is melted in water and cools, it forms a gel. Scientists call this gel a colloid, and it can refract and reflect light in an interesting way.

The word *refraction* refers to the way light changes speed and direction when it moves through different transparent materials, such as air, oil, water, and even gelatin.

When light waves hit the gelatin in mirror glaze, they are bent and reflected in a way that gives the glaze a glossy, reflective appearance.

9. When you're done, put the desserts in the refrigerator, uncovered, for 1–2 hours to harden the glaze.

10. Present your culinary creation. **(Fig. 6)**

CREATE AND COMBINE

Coat chocolate cupcakes (Lab 34), chocolate mousse (Lab 45), or perfect layer cake (Lab 33) with mirror glaze.

Make colorful meringue mushrooms (Lab 48) to top off your mirrored masterpieces.

OLD-FASHIONED PUDDING

INGREDIENTS

→ 2 tablespoons cornstarch

→ ¾ cup (150 g) sugar (use brown sugar (112.5 g) for butterscotch pudding)

→ ¼ teaspoon salt

→ 2 slightly beaten egg yolks

→ 2 cups (475 ml) milk

→ 2 tablespoons (28 g) butter (3 tablespoons, or 42 g, if using brown sugar)

→ 1½ teaspoon (7.5 ml) vanilla extract

EQUIPMENT

→ Ladle (optional)

→ Medium or large pot with heavy bottom

→ Sieve, sifter, or pan-safe fork

→ Small bowl

→ Stove

→ Wire whisk

SAFETY TIPS AND HINTS

If using brown sugar, increase the amount of butter to 3 tablespoons (42 g)

CHALLENGE LEVEL	ALLERGEN ALERTS Dairy, eggs	TIME 30 minutes, plus cooling time	YIELD Around 3 cups (675 g)

THERE'S SOMETHING COMFORTING ABOUT PUDDING. THIS MIDWESTERN RECIPE CAN BE MADE WITH OR WITHOUT BROWN SUGAR, DEPENDING ON WHETHER YOU WANT BUTTERSCOTCH OR VANILLA. GOBBLE IT UP, OR USE IT TO FILL A PIE CRUST.

Fig. 5: Enjoy your old-fashioned pudding.

Fig. 1: Whisk egg yolks with warm milk.

Fig. 2: Add the egg mixture into the pan.

Fig. 3: Blend in the butter.

Fig. 4: Ladle into custard bowls.

THE SCIENCE
BEHIND THE FOOD:

Starches, such as cornstarch, are made from dried, shrunken plant cells that are really good at soaking up water.

If you heat corn starch in water, you can see the solution thicken and become more transparent as the granules swell up with water. The swollen starch looks clear when light moves through it at the same speed and angle it's moving through the water. Scientist call this change gelatinization.

During the next phase, which is called pasting, the starch starts shedding molecules that make the liquid they're suspended in thicken dramatically when it cools down. That's why pudding thickens as it cools.

RECIPE

1. Sift dry ingredients into a medium saucepan or pot, or add them and mix well using a fork.

2. Add the milk and stir over medium heat until the mixture thickens. When it bubbles, stir for 2 more minutes before removing it from the heat.

3. Put the egg yolks in a small bowl and ladle in some of the hot milk mixture. Whisk to combine well. **(Fig. 1)**

4. Scrape the warm egg yolk mixture back into the pan and whisk it to blend. Cook over medium heat for 2 more minutes, stirring. **(Fig. 2)**

5. Remove the mixture from the heat and blend in the butter and vanilla. **(Fig. 3)**

6. Ladle or pour the pudding into individual dishes or a prebaked pie crust. It will thicken as it cools. **(Fig. 4)**

7. Enjoy! **(Fig. 5)**

CREATE AND COMBINE
Make and bake a pie crust (Lab 37) to fill with vanilla pudding and top the pie with fruit.

Homemade whipped cream (Lab 39) makes pudding even better!

LUSCIOUS LEMON CURD

INGREDIENTS

→ 3 lemons (¼ to ½ cup juice, depending on the size of the lemons)

→ 1 cup (200 g) sugar

→ ½ cup (112 g) salted butter

→ 3 eggs

EQUIPMENT

→ Juicer or citrus press

→ Medium saucepan with heavy bottom

→ Sieve (optional)

→ Spoon

→ Stove

→ Wire whisk

→ Zester, fine cheese grater, or a microplane grater

SAFETY TIPS AND HINTS

Don't add the eggs to the juice, butter, and syrup if the mixture too hot—the eggs will cook.

You can leave the zest in the curd, but I prefer it smooth, so I suggest straining it before eating and storing.

CHALLENGE LEVEL	ALLERGEN ALERTS	TIME	YIELD
🎩🎩	Dairy, eggs	30 minutes, plus cooling time	Around 2 cups (500g)

LEMON CURD IS EYE CANDY FOR CITRUS LOVERS AND MAKES A PERFECT FILLING FOR ANGEL FOOD CAKE OR CREAM PUFFS. SMOOTH AND CREAMY, IT HAS AN INTENSE LEMON ZING THAT INSTANTLY BRIGHTENS ANY PASTRY, BUT YOU MAY JUST WANT TO EAT IT BY THE SPOONFUL.

Adapted from Mark Bittman's *How to Cook Everything*.

Fig. 5: Fill cream puffs with lemon curd and whipped cream.

Fig. 1: Add lemon zest to sauce pan.

Fig. 2: Add lemon juice, butter, and sugar to the pan.

Fig. 3: Whisk in the eggs.

Fig. 4: Spoon into jars.

Fig. 6: Lemon curd and whipped cream makes a delicious cake filling.

RECIPE

1. Wash the lemons well and zest one of them using a zester or grater. Add the zest to the sauce pan. **(Fig. 1)**

2. Cut the lemons in half and juice them.

3. Add the lemon juice, butter, and sugar to the lemon zest in the saucepan. **(Fig. 2)**

4. Place the pan on the stove and stir over very low heat until the sugar is mostly dissolved and the butter has melted.

5. When the last piece of butter has just melted away, whisk the eggs, one at a time, into the warm sugar mixture. Alternately, premix the eggs and whisk them in all at once. **(Fig. 3)**

6. Keep cooking over medium-low heat, stirring continuously, for 10-20 minutes until the mixture thickens to the consistency of thin pudding. Don't let it boil or the proteins in the eggs will denature (permanently unwind) and you'll get lumps.

7. Strain the curd through a sieve to remove the lemon zest (optional).

8. Let it cool for 5 minutes and then pour it into storage jars or serving containers, such as small bowls or ramekins. **(Fig. 4)**

THE SCIENCE BEHIND THE FOOD:

Chefs use the word "curdled" to describe the situation when the fats and proteins have separated out into curds (lumps.) Ironically, despite its name, you don't want any curds or clumps in lemon curd, which should be a smooth, thick, creamy spread.

Lemon curd is made using two components that can ruin its smooth texture: acid and heat. Both can denature, or irreversibly unwind, egg proteins to create lumps of scrambled egg. By dissolving sugar in lemon juice and combining it with the fat in melted butter, you create an environment where egg proteins can unwind a little and interact to thicken the mixture, but not denature completely to form lumps.

9. Eat the lemon curd straight from the bowl, spread it on a scone, or use it as cake or cream puff filling. **(Fig. 5, 6)**

CREATE AND COMBINE
Lemon curd pairs perfectly with angel food cake (Lab 35) and cream puffs (Lab 38).

MELTINGLY MARVELOUS MOUSSE

INGREDIENTS

→ 16 ounces (455 g) good-quality bittersweet chocolate

→ 2 eggs

→ 4 egg yolks

→ 4 egg whites (see Hints)

→ 2 cups (475 ml) cream

→ 6 tablespoons (45 g) powdered (confectioners') sugar

→ Chocolate wafers or chocolate sandwich cookies (optional)

→ Gummy worms (optional)

EQUIPMENT

→ Double boiler or one larger and one smaller pan

→ Mixing bowls

→ Spoon

→ Stand or hand mixer

→ Stove

→ Whisk

CHALLENGE LEVEL ♟♟♟	ALLERGEN ALERTS Dairy, eggs	TIME 45 minutes	YIELD 6–8 cups (2.5–3 kg)

Fig. 8: Or layer with crumbs and gummy worms.

THIS CHOCOLATE MOUSSE IS MY FAVORITE. PAIR IT WITH WHIPPED CREAM TO MAKE IT FANCY, OR WITH CRUSHED CHOCOLATE COOKIES AND GUMMY WORMS TO MAKE IT FUN.

Adapted from a recipe by Donna Nordin for chocolate mousse pie.

Fig. 1: Chop the chocolate.

Fig. 2: Melt the chocolate.

Fig. 3: Whisk in the egg yolks.

SAFETY TIPS AND HINTS

This recipe contains raw egg whites. I recommend using pasteurized eggs or coddling your own eggs (Lab 16) to ensure the mousse is safe to eat. Refrigerate any leftovers.

Don't overbeat the egg whites. They should be stiff, but not dry.

RECIPE

1. If using chocolate sandwich cookies, scrape the filling out. Crush the cookies or wafers.

2. Chop the chocolate into tiny pieces so that it will melt more quickly. **(Fig. 1)**

3. Melt the chocolate in a double-boiler or in a pan set over a larger pan of simmering water. Once melted, remove from the heat and cool for 10 minutes or so. **(Fig. 2)**

4. Whisk 2 whole eggs into the chocolate and mix well. **(Fig. 3)**

5. Add the 4 egg yolks and mix again until completely combined.

6. In a separate bowl, use a mixer to whip the cream and powdered sugar until soft peaks form. **(Fig. 4)**

7. Use a third bowl to beat the whites of 4 eggs until they form stiff, glossy peaks but are not dry. **(Fig. 5)**

8. Stir ¼ of the whipped cream and ¼ of the beaten egg whites into the chocolate mixture.

9. Gently fold in the rest of the whipped cream and egg whites, a little at a time, being careful not to destroy the foams. **(Fig. 6)**

10. Spoon the mousse into bowls and serve it with whipped cream and chocolate wafers or layer it with wafer crumbs and gummy worms in a clear glass. **(Fig. 7, 8, 9)**

CREATE AND COMBINE

Make a chocolate bowl or dome (Lab 47) for chocolate mousse or top it with some homemade whipped cream (Lab 39).

MELTINGLY MARVELOUS MOUSSE (CONTINUED)

Fig. 4: Whip the cream.

Fig. 5: Beat the egg whites.

Fig. 6: Alternate folding in cream and eggs.

Fig. 7: Serve the mousse with whipped cream.

Fig. 9: Crushed wafers are delicious.

Fig. 10: Yum!

THE SCIENCE
BEHIND THE FOOD:

Comminution is the act of reducing a material to minute particles or fragments.

When melting chocolate, comminution comes in handy. Breaking material into lots of little pieces dramatically increases its surface area, which allows heat to come into contact with more chocolate all at once, melting it more quickly and evenly.

The air bubbles created by whipping cream and egg whites give the chocolate mousse a beautiful texture that makes it feels smooth and light in your mouth.

DARING DECORATIONS AND DELECTABLE DESSERTS

MAKE DESSERTS EXTRA SPECIAL BY DECKING THEM OUT WITH GLASS-PHASE SUGAR FOAM, AMORPHOUS CANDY, AND DISORDERED BUTTERFAT. In other words, with some candy science, you can top cakes with spectacular meringue mushrooms, cover a cupcake with fondant, craft custom homemade marshmallows, and dip photo-worthy chocolate domes and bowls on balloons.

Creating smooth, cold, perfect frozen treats is a balancing act, and the secret is in the ice. Every scrumptious scoop of ice cream, frozen custard, gelato, or sorbet contains a mouthful of science, since three phases of matter coexist in every bite. Under a microscope, frozen treats appear as bubbles and ice crystals suspended in a liquid sugar-syrup goo.

Milk, cream, and any fruit added to the mixture all contribute water to make frozen crystals in ice cream. Sugar, salt, and gelatin act as antifreeze agents, physically getting in the way of ice crystal formation to keep crystals small so that you don't end up with one big chunk of ice.

Ideally, a frozen dessert feels cold and smooth in your mouth, its ice crystals are very small, and there are just enough bubbles to keep it scoopable but not too frothy.

"Ice cream is popular because of its mouthfeel, conveying a sensation of decadence on the tongue."

Elke Scholten and Miriam Peters, from *The Kitchen as Laboratory: Reflections on the Science of Food and Cooking* by Cesar Vega, Job Ubbink, and Erik van der Linden

FABULOUS FONDANT

INGREDIENTS

→ ½ ounce good white baking chocolate containing cocoa butter

→ 3 cups (150 g) small marshmallows

→ 1 tablespoon (14 g) butter, cut up

→ 1½ teaspoons (7.5 ml) milk

→ 1 teaspoon (5 ml) clear vanilla extract (or other clear flavoring, depending on use)

→ 1½ cups (180 g) powdered (confectioners') sugar, plus more for kneading

→ Food coloring (gel works best, but liquid is fine)

EQUIPMENT

→ Cutting board

→ Knife

→ Medium-sized microwavable bowl

→ Microwave oven

→ Mixing spoon

→ Rolling pin

CHALLENGE LEVEL	ALLERGEN ALERTS Dairy	TIME 30 minutes	YIELD 3-4 8-inch (20 cm) round sheets of fondant, ⅛ inch (3 mm) thick

FONDANT IS ESSENTIALLY EDIBLE PLAY DOUGH THAT CAN BE ROLLED INTO SMOOTH SHEETS TO COVER A CAKE, CUT INTO SHAPES, OR SCULPTED INTO AMAZING FIGURES. BETTER YET, YOU CAN MAKE IT IN THE MICROWAVE USING MARSHMALLOWS AND MIX YOUR FAVORITE COLORS.

Adapted from the *Better Homes & Gardens* Blog.

Fig. 5: Cut shapes out.

SAFETY TIPS AND HINTS

Adult supervisiom reccomended for microwaving chocolate and marshmallows.

Fig. 1: Melt the marshmallows, butter, milk, and white chocolate.

Fig. 2: Remove the mixture from the bowl.

Fig. 3: Knead with powdered sugar.

Fig. 4: Tint with food coloring.

Fig. 6: What else could you make?

RECIPE

1. Chop the white chocolate into small pieces.

2. Combine the chopped chocolate, marshmallows, butter, and milk in the microwavable bowl. Microwave on high for 1 minute and stir until smooth. If needed, microwave for 30 more seconds until everything is melted. **(Fig. 1)**

3. Stir in the vanilla and mix well.

4. Add the powdered sugar and stir to combine.

5. Sprinkle a smooth, flat work surface with ½ cup (60 g) powdered sugar and scrape the marshmallow mixture onto the sugar-coated surface. **(Fig. 2)**

6. Dust the marshmallow mix with powdered sugar and knead it, incorporating more powdered sugar until it is no longer sticky. It will probably take 5–10 minutes of kneading. **(Fig. 3)**

7. Use food coloring to tint the fondant by kneading the color in. You can make it all one color or divide it into multiple batches and make lots of colors. **(Fig. 4)**

8. Use the fondant immediately by rolling it out to about ⅛ inch (3 mm) thick to cut and sculpt immediately or store it in plastic wrap. It dries out quickly, so it's best to roll it and wrap it in plastic until you're ready to cut or sculpt it. **(Fig. 5, 6)**

9. Fondant can be stored for 1–2 weeks at room temperature, tightly wrapped.

CREATE AND COMBINE

Use fondant to decorate chocolate cupcakes (Lab 34) or be bold and use it to cover a layer cake (Lab 33). Remember to prefrost cakes with buttercream (Lab 40) to keep rolled fondant looking smooth.

THE SCIENCE
BEHIND THE FOOD:

Fondant can be stored at room temperature for a week or more because it's so sweet.

Corn syrup and sugar make it almost impossible for bacteria to grow. Sweet solutions put osmotic pressure on bacteria by pulling water out of them and making it difficult for them to collect the water and nutrients they need to survive.

High sugar content is the reason you don't have to refrigerate things such as honey and syrup. Salt also puts osmotic pressure on bacteria and has been used as a preservative for thousands of years.

CHOCOLATE DOMES AND BOWLS

INGREDIENTS

→ 12 ounces, or 4 cups (340 g) semisweet chocolate

→ 4 ounces (115 g) white chocolate

→ Sprinkles (optional)

EQUIPMENT

→ 10–12 round (5-inch [13 cm]) balloons

→ Baking sheet

→ Bowl slightly larger in diameter than inflated balloons

→ Freezer with space cleared for balloons

→ Microwave oven or stove

→ Microwave-safe bowl, double boiler, or one larger and one smaller pan

→ Pastry bag or plastic zipper bag with one corner cut off

→ Small glasses or ramekins

→ Spoon

SAFETY TIPS AND HINTS

Don't get the chocolate too hot or it will melt the balloons.

Don't serve to anyone with a latex allergy.

CHALLENGE LEVEL	ALLERGEN ALERTS Dairy	TIME 30 minutes, plus 30 minutes in the freezer	YIELD 10–12 domes or bowls

GRAB SOME SMALL BALLOONS AND CLEAR A SPACE IN YOUR FREEZER TO MAKE BEAUTIFUL, VERSATILE CHOCOLATE DOMES. EDIBLE BOWLS CAN BE TRANSFORMED INTO EYE CANDY WITH WHITE CHOCOLATE DRIZZLES OR A FEW SPRINKLES.

Fig. 5: Use as a bowl or a dome.

RECIPE

1. Blow up the balloons. Set glasses or ramekins on the baking sheet.

2. Chop the semisweet chocolate into small pieces.

3. Melt the chocolate in the microwave for 30 seconds at a time, stirring for 30 seconds between each heating until just melted and smooth. Alternately, melt the chocolate in a pan over a larger pan of simmering water. The chocolate should not be too hot.

4. Repeat Steps 2 and 3 with the white chocolate.

5. Put the semisweet chocolate in the bowl slightly larger than the balloons and dip the untied end of a balloon in, coating the lower third of the balloon with chocolate. **(Fig. 1)**

6. Flip the balloon over onto a ramekin or small glass to cool.

7. Spoon some melted white chocolate into the plastic zipper bag and pipe it over the chocolate on the balloon (optional).

8. Add sprinkles if you wish. Dip the rest of the balloons, reheating the chocolate if necessary. **(Fig. 2)**

9. Put the balloons in the freezer until they're solid and you're ready to eat them. **(Fig. 3)**

10. Remove chocolate domes from the freezer. Pop the balloons and slowly pull them out of the domes. **(Fig. 4)**

11. Use the domes as bowls, filled with ice cream, or flip them over and hide a treat underneath. **(Fig. 5)**

CREATE AND COMBINE

Fill a dome or bowl with chocolate mousse (Lab 45) or homemade ice cream (Lab 50).

Like drama? Make chocolate ganache (Lab 41) with a little extra cream. Be sure it's hot and pour it over the dome to melt it, revealing a treat you've hidden underneath.

THE SCIENCE
BEHIND THE FOOD:

You may have noticed that good (often more expensive) dark, bittersweet, or semisweet chocolate is glossy, breaks with a crisp snap when you bite it, and feels smooth in your mouth. Lower-quality chocolate can be dull and soft. How chocolate looks and feels in your mouth depends on what's been added to it and how it's been treated.

Cocoa butter gives chocolate its physical structure. This fat can be cajoled into a perfect crystalline structure in a method called tempering, which involves controlled heating and cooling of the chocolate to destroy unwanted crystals and encourage formation of more orderly crystals, which look shiny.

Melting chocolate, using it to coat balloons, and cooling it in the freezer will probably destroy the tempered structure of whatever chocolate you use, but starting with good chocolate will always give you tastier results.

Fig. 1: Dip the balloons in the melted chocolate.

Fig. 2: Add white chocolate and sprinkles.

Fig. 3: Freeze the chocolate.

Fig. 4: Remove from the freezer.

MERINGUE MUSHROOMS

INGREDIENTS

→ 3 egg whites (room temperature)

→ ¼ teaspoon cream of tartar

→ ½ cup (100 g) granulated sugar

→ ¼ teaspoon (1.25 ml) vanilla extract

→ Food coloring (gel works best)

→ Dusting sugar (optional)

EQUIPMENT

→ ½-inch (1 cm) round piping tip for pastry bag or plastic bag

→ 2 baking sheets

→ Oven

→ Parchment paper

→ Pastry bag or large plastic zipper bag with one corner cut off

→ Stand mixer or hand mixer and stainless steel bowl

→ Toothpicks

→ Metal mixing bowl

CHALLENGE LEVEL	ALLERGEN ALERTS	TIME	YIELD
	Eggs	30 minutes, plus 2-3 hours to bake	2 dozen mushrooms

THESE PRETTY LITTLE MERINGUES TASTE AS GOOD AS THEY LOOK. PIPE THEM OUT WITH STREAKS OF FOOD COLORING AND DUST THEM WITH SOME SHIMMERING SUGAR TO CREATE PURE CULINARY MAGIC.

Fig. 6: Use meringues to decorate a cake.

RECIPE

1. Preheat the oven to 200°F (93°C).

2. Line the baking sheets with parchment paper.

3. Beat 3 egg whites on medium until they foam.

4. Add the cream of tartar and continue to beat, increasing the speed to high. **(Fig. 1)**

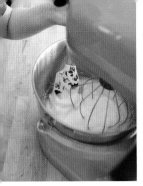

Fig. 1: Beat the egg whites.

Fig. 2: Pipe caps for the mushrooms.

Fig. 3: Pipe stems.

Fig. 4: Dust the caps with sugar.

Fig. 5: Add stems to the mushrooms caps.

SAFETY TIPS AND HINTS

Don't skip the cream of tartar. It helps stabilize the egg whites in the meringue.

The general recipe for meringues is around ¼ cup (56 g) sugar per egg white, with a pinch of cream of tartar.

5. When soft peaks form, add the sugar 1 tablespoon (13 g) or so at a time as you beat the eggs. Add the vanilla.

6. Continue beating the mixture until stiff, glossy peaks with rounded tips form. Don't overbeat.

7. Add a ½-inch tip to the pastry or plastic bag. Fill the bag with the meringue you've made.

8. Make some colorful streaks on the meringue by using a toothpick to smear food coloring on the inside of the pastry tip or bag before piping.

9. Pipe half of the meringue into blobs that look like mushroom caps on one of the baking sheets. **(Fig. 2)**

10. With the other half of the meringue, make pointed stems, each around 1 inch tall. They don't have to be perfect! **(Fig. 3)**

11. Leave the mushrooms caps alone or dust them with tinted sugar. **(Fig. 4)**

12. Save any meringue left in the bowl and pastry bag to use as glue when you assemble the meringues.

13. Bake the meringues for 1–2 hours, until they feel dry, then remove them from the oven and let them cool.

14. Poke a small hole in the bottom of each mushroom cap, smear some meringue on the broken spots, and insert the pointy side of one of the stems. Put them back in the oven at 200°F (93°C) for 15 minutes to set the meringue. **(Fig. 5)**

15. Eat your confectionary creations or use them to decorate a cake. **(Fig. 6)**

CREATE AND COMBINE
Use your mushrooms to decorate a Tie-Dye Roll Cake (Lab 36), some crazy-good chocolate cupcakes (Lab 34), or pair them up with some berries on an angel food cake (Lab 35) to create a botanical theme.

THE SCIENCE BEHIND THE FOOD:

Meringues are egg whites whipped into sugary foams. They can be soft or hard, depending on how long they're baked, and hard meringues contain more sugar.

As you whip air into the mix, egg-white proteins stick to the bubbles, stabilizing them so that they form a thick foam. The sugar you add combines with water from the eggs to form sweet syrup.

Baking the meringue at a low temperature for a long period of time transforms the sugar and protein from an elastic goo to a solid foam in a glassy state, creating a sweet, brittle network of bubbles.

MARVELOUS MARSHMALLOWS

INGREDIENTS

→ Oil or clear cooking spray

→ 3 ¼ ounce (7.5 g) envelopes of unflavored gelatin

→ 1 cup (235 ml) water

→ 1 cup (235 ml) light corn syrup

→ 1 ½ cups (300 g) granulated sugar

→ Powdered (confectioners') sugar (for dusting the baking pan)

→ ¼ teaspoon salt

→ 1 teaspoon (5 ml) peppermint extract or 2 teaspoons (10 ml) pure vanilla extract

EQUIPMENT

→ 10-inch (25 cm) square baking pan

→ Butter knife

→ Candy thermometer

→ Cutting board

→ Heavy saucepan

→ Mixing spoon

→ Oven

→ Sieve or sifter

→ Spatula (optional)

→ Stand mixer or hand mixer and bowl

CHALLENGE LEVEL	TIME 30 minutes, plus cooling time	YIELD 10-inch (25 cm) square pan of marshmallows

CREATE DELICIOUS HANDMADE MARSHMALLOWS USING SUGAR, CORN SYRUP, AND UNFLAVORED GELATIN.

Adapted from *epicurious.com*.

Fig. 4: Decorate the marshmallows.

SAFETY TIPS AND HINTS

Sugar syrup can cause dangerous burns, so an adult should supervise at all times and handle hot syrup.

Gelatin can have an unpleasant smell. Adding flavor such as peppermint or vanilla to the marshmallows will make them taste and smell good.

Yellow cooking spray or oil will work, but it discolors the marshmallows.

RECIPE

1. Oil the baking pan and coat it with powdered sugar using the sieve or sifter.

2. Add the gelatin packets to ½ cup (120 ml) water in your mixing bowl. Stir it well and let it sit in order to hydrate (add water to) the gelatin.

3. In the saucepan, combine the corn syrup, sugar, remaining water, and salt. Bring the mixture to a boil over medium heat, stirring.

4. Carefully, put a candy thermometer into the hot syrup and continue boiling without stirring until it reaches the soft-ball stage (240°F/116°C), as indicated by the candy thermometer. Alternately, add a drop of the hot syrup to a glass of cold water. When it just holds its shape, it is at the soft-ball stage. **(Fig. 1)**

5. Remove the pan from the heat and let cool for 5 minutes.

6. Turn the mixer on low. Slowly and very carefully, pour the hot syrup down the side of the bowl into the gelatin and water.

7. Once all of the syrup has been added, increase the mixer speed to high and beat for 5 minutes, or until the marshmallow is thick enough to form ribbons. **(Fig. 2)**

8. Add vanilla or peppermint extract to the marshmallow and beat it briefly.

9. Pour the marshmallow into the baking pan that you coated with powdered sugar. Use a wet spatula to flatten and smooth the surface of the marshmallow. Let it cool.

10. To remove the marshmallows from the pan, use a butter knife to loosen the sides. Invert (flip) the pan onto a cutting board coated with powdered sugar.

11. Oil the knife and coat it with sugar to cut the marshmallow into smaller pieces. **(Fig. 3)**

12. Decorate the marshmallows using granulated sugar, colorful dusting sugars, or sprinkles. **(Fig. 4)**

13. Taste your marvelous marshmallows. **(Fig. 5)**

CREATE AND COMBINE
Color the marshmallows or make them thinner by pouring them into a larger pan so you can use cookie cutters dipped in powdered sugar to cut out fun shapes.

Make hot chocolate to go with your marshmallows.

Fig. 1: Boil the syrup until it reaches the soft-ball stage.

Fig. 2: Beat until the marshmallow forms thick ribbons.

Fig. 3: Cut the marshmallows using an oiled knife.

Fig. 5: Taste your homemade marshmallows.

THE SCIENCE
BEHIND THE FOOD:

Soft and chewy candies, such as marshmallows, are called amorphous or noncrystalline candies.

Beating hot sugar syrup together with gelatin and water creates air bubbles. As the foam cools, corn syrup interferes with crystal formation and the gelatin turns from a liquid into a gel, trapping bubbles inside.

Adding marshmallows to hot chocolate causes the gelatin to melt again, turning them back into sugar syrup.

EASY ICE CREAM

INGREDIENTS

→ 1 cup (250 ml) whole milk

→ ¾ cup (150 g) sugar

→ 1 teaspoon (5 ml) vanilla extract

→ ⅛ teaspoon salt

→ 2 cups (500 ml) heavy whipping cream

→ 5 large egg yolks

EQUIPMENT

→ Large bowl filled with ice

→ Large, flat dish, such as a casserole dish or cake pan

→ Mixing spoon

→ Small or medium saucepan with a heavy bottom

→ Strainer and bowl that fits under strainer

→ Spatula (optional)

→ Whisk

CHALLENGE LEVEL	ALLERGEN ALERTS Dairy, eggs	TIME 30 minutes hands-on, plus several hours to freeze	YIELD 1 quart (570 g) ice cream

YOU DON'T NEED AN ICE CREAM MAKER TO CREATE DELICIOUS HOMEMADE ICE CREAM. WITH A FREEZER AND SOME PATIENCE, IT'S EASY TO MAKE THIS DELICIOUS CUSTARD-BASED FROZEN TREAT.

Adapted from *The Perfect Scoop* by David Lebovitz.

Fig. 6: Add ganache (Lab 41) for panache.

Fig. 1: Seperate the egg whites from the egg yolks.

Fig. 2: Measure the cream into the bowl under the strainer.

Fig. 3: Strain the custard into the cream.

Fig. 4: Pour into the shallow dish, place in the freezer, and stir often.

Fig. 5: Scoop and enjoy.

RECIPE

1. Pour the milk, sugar, and salt into the saucepan. Heat to 120°F (49°C) while stirring, and remove the pan from the heat.

2. Seperate yolks from whites. In a separate bowl, mix the egg yolks together until smooth. Whisk ½ cup (120 ml) of the milk mixture into the egg yolks. **(Fig. 1)**

3. Scrape and mix the warmed egg yolks into the rest of the milk mixture in the pan and cook the mixture at low heat until it coats the spoon (around 180°F/82°C). This is your custard.

4. Complete the ice cream mixture by adding the heavy whipping cream and vanilla to the bowl under the strainer. Strain the custard into the cream and mix well. **(Fig. 2, 3)**

5. Put the bowl of ice cream mix over an ice-filled bowl, stirring to chill.

6. Transfer the ice cream mixture to your large, flat dish. **(Fig. 4)**

7. Put the dish in the freezer and stir it every 15 minutes or so until it is completely frozen. Be sure to scrape down the sides and mix it well each time you stir.

8. Enjoy your homemade ice cream! **(Fig. 5, 6)**

CREATE AND COMBINE

Serve homemade ice cream with any of the Bossy Cakes (Course 7) or Daring Desserts (Course 8) in this book.

There's nothing better than homemade ice cream with hot fudge sauce (ganache, Lab 41).

THE SCIENCE
BEHIND THE FOOD:

Surrounding ice cream mixture with very cold temperatures allows the water in the mix to begin freezing. Solid ice crystals form, liquid water disappears, and the sugar concentration in the mixture increases, creating a syrupy base as the ice cream thickens.

Stirring or whipping the ice cream mixture adds air to the concoction and breaks up large crystals. Milk fats and proteins provide support for bubbles. The alcohol in vanilla, and other additions, keep crystals tiny, which makes the ice cream feel smooth and cold in your mouth.

BREATHTAKING BAKED ALASKA

INGREDIENTS

→ 1 graham cracker or chocolate wafer crust

→ 1 quart (570 g) ice cream

→ Topping for ice cream, such as fresh fruit or chocolate chips

→ 5 egg whites (room temperature)

→ ½ cup plus 2 tablespoons (100 g) sugar

→ ½ teaspoon cream of tartar

EQUIPMENT

→ Oven

→ Plastic wrap

→ Stand or hand mixer

→ Whisk

→ Metal mixing bowl

→ Freezer

CHALLENGE LEVEL	ALLERGEN ALERTS	TIME	YIELD
♟♟♟	Dairy, eggs, wheat	30 minutes hands-on, plus 5 minutes to bake	1 large pie

Fig. 6: Bake until golden and dig in right away.

A MOUND OF COLD ICE CREAM MAKES A TASTY BASE FOR A MOUNTAIN OF PERFECTLY BAKED MERINGUE. THIS SIMPLE VERSION OF A SHOW-STOPPING DESSERT DEMONSTRATES THAT WHIPPED EGG WHITES MAKE SPECTACULAR AND EFFECTIVE INSULATION.

Adapted from Ina Garten's Baked Alaska recipe.

RECIPE

Cut the ice cream into slabs to fill the pie crust.

. Fill the pie crust with ice cream, pack it down, cover with plastic wrap, and freeze until you're ready to bake the meringue. **(Fig. 1)**

. Preheat the oven to 400°F (200°C).

. Whisk the egg whites until they start to foam. Add the cream of tartar and continue whipping until soft peaks form. Add the sugar, 1 tablespoon (13 g) at a time, as you continue beating.

. Beat the meringue until you have glossy, stiff peaks with rounded tops. **(Fig. 2)**

THE SCIENCE
BEHIND THE FOOD:

The meringue on a baked Alaska is a foam made up of too many bubbles to count, which makes it a perfect, edible, insulator.

Without meringue, heat from the oven would move quickly to the ice cream, increasing its temperature and melting it. However, the network of air-filled bubbles in meringue slows heat transfer, acting as an insulator, to keep the ice cream frozen.

SAFETY TIPS AND HINTS

Some of the egg whites in the center of the meringue may not cook completely. You can make the same recipe using pasteurized eggs, but the meringue may not whip up as high.

You'll want to serve this dessert immediately after baking, so plan ahead! Ice cream can be frozen into the pie crust in advance and covered with plastic wrap.

6. Take out the ice cream pie and add a thin layer of fruit or chocolate chips. **(Fig. 3, 4)**

7. Pile the meringue on the pie, sealing around the edges. Make it look pretty and pop it in the oven for 5 minutes, or until golden brown. Serve immediately. **(Fig. 5, 6)**

CREATE AND COMBINE

This dessert stands on its own, but every dessert is better with some hot fudge (Lab 41) drizzled over the top.

Fig. 1: Fill the pie crust with ice cream.   *Fig. 2: Make meringue.*

Fig. 4: Chocolate chips are good on ice cream too!

Fig. 3: Cover the pie crust with fruit.   *Fig. 5: Sculpt the meringue.*

SCRUMPTIOUS SORBET

INGREDIENTS

- → 1 pound (455 g) fresh strawberries
- → 1 cup (200 g) sugar
- → ½ cup (120 ml) water
- → ¼ cup (60 ml) lemon juice
- → ⅛ teaspoon salt

EQUIPMENT

- → Knife
- → Juicer or citrus press
- → Large, flat dish for freezing sorbet
- → Medium saucepan
- → Stove

CHALLENGE LEVEL	TIME	YIELD
♟♟	30 minutes hands-on, plus several hours in the freezer	Around 1 quart (570 g)

SWEET AND INTENSELY FLAVORED ICE CRYSTALS INTERMINGLE TO CREATE THIS DELIGHTFUL DAIRY-FREE DESSERT THAT YOU CAN BLEND IT UP IN NO TIME. POP IT IN THE FREEZER TO MIX UP COLD, CRYSTALLINE PERFECTION.

Adapted from *Cook's Illustrated*.

Fig. 4: Put the mixture in a flat dish in the freezer.

RECIPE

Cut the strawberries, removing all tops, and juice the lemons. (Fig. 1, 2)

Make a sugar syrup: mix the sugar, water, lemon juice, and a salt in the saucepan.

Bring the mixture to a boil over medium-high heat.

Remove the sugar syrup from the heat and allow it to cool.

Place the strawberries in a blender and blend them until smooth.

Pour the cooled sugar syrup into the blender and blend it with the strawberries. **(Fig. 3)**

Pour the mixture into the shallow dish and place it in the freezer, stirring every 30 minutes until smooth. Repeat until the sorbet is completely frozen. **(Fig. 4, 5)**

CREATE AND COMBINE

Strawberry sorbet is good on its own, but its intense fruit flavor also tastes amazing with angel food cake (Lab 35) and cream puffs (Lab 38).

Fig. 1: Clean and cut the fruit.

Fig. 2: Juice the lemons.

Fig. 3: Blend until smooth.

Fig. 5: Stir well each time it starts to freeze.

THE SCIENCE BEHIND THE FOOD:

Sorbet is a nondairy, fruit-based dessert. The main difference between sorbet and ice cream is how much air is incorporated into the frozen mix.

While ice cream has egg to keep bubbles intact, sorbet lacks such proteins. Gelatin can be added to stabilize sorbet, and many fruits contain pectin, which forms a gel that can thicken sorbet.

Fig. 6: Enjoy every chilly mouthful of sorbet.

ABOUT

ABOUT THE AUTHOR

Liz Heinecke has loved science since she was old enough to inspect her first caterpillar. After working in molecular biology research for ten years, she left the lab to kick off a new chapter in her life as a stay-at-home mom. Soon she found herself sharing her love of science with her three kids and journaling their experiments and adventures on her Kitchen Pantry Scientist website.

These days, Liz appears regularly on television, makes science videos, and writes about science online and in books. Liz's work includes *Kitchen Science Lab for Kids*, *Outdoor Science Lab for Kids*, *STEAM Lab for Kids*, and *Star Wars Maker Lab*. When she's not driving her kids around and doing science outreach, you'll find Liz at home in Minnesota, singing, playing banjo, painting, running, and doing almost anything else to avoid housework.

Liz graduated from Luther College, where she studied art and biology. She received her master's degree in bacteriology from the University of Wisconsin, Madison.

ABOUT THE PHOTOGRAPHER

Amber Procaccini is a commercial and editorial photographer based in Minneapolis, Minnesota. She specializes in photographing kids, babies, food, and travel, and her passion for photography almost equals her passion for finding the perfect taco. Amber met Liz while photographing Liz's first book, *Kitchen Science Lab for Kids*, and she knew they'd make a great team when they bonded over cornichons, pâté, and brie. When Amber isn't photographing eye-rolling tweens or making cheeseburgers look sexy, she and her husband love to travel and enjoy new adventures together.

Abigail	Addie	Alessa	Ara	Aryanna	Audrey	Berit	Bridget
Carissa	Claire	Claire	Connor	Darya	Delaney	Divya	Easton
Eden	Elizabeth	Elizabeth	Evan	Georgia	Grace	Grace	Grady
Gunnar	Haakon	Harper	Henry	Ingrid	Jace	Jack	Jasper
John	Katy	Keya	Khalil	Kirin	Kyra	Leah	Leo
Lila	Lucy	Maria	May	McKenna	Mia	Mikaylah	Miles
Olivia	Olivia	Peter	Roxie	Ryan	Samuel	Sanna	Sarah
Scarlett	Sean	Sonja	Soren	Stella	Will	Wyatt	Zayna

INDEX